MusicNotes

A Note-taking Companion for

FOURTH EDITION

Understanding Music

JEREMY YUDKIN

BOSTON UNIVERSITY

PEARSON
Prentice
Hall

Upper Saddle River, NJ 07458

© 2005 by Pearson Education, Inc.
Upper Saddle River, New Jersey 07458

10 9 8 7 6 5 4 3 2 1

ISBN 0-13-150560-2

Printed in the United States of America

PEARSON
Prentice
Hall

Contents

MusicNotes

A Note-taking Companion for

Understanding Music

Listening Sketch for Shakuhachi Music
Koku-Reibo **(A Bell Ringing in the**
      Empty Sky)

Duration: 4:27

Student CD Collection: 1, track 1
Complete CD Collection: 1, track 1

*T*he shakuhachi is a bamboo flute with five finger holes and is blown from one end. Its name means "one and eight-tenths," because in Japanese measurement the shakuhachi has the length of one and eight-tenths *shaku* (a shaku is roughly a foot).

Music for the shakuhachi has a profound, mystical quality. The instrument was used as part of religious ceremony by Zen Buddhist monks in the seventeenth century, and it has been said that a single note of the shakuhachi can bring one to the state of nirvana (perfect blessedness).

The piece that we shall hear is one of the oldest in the repertory, dating back to the seventeenth century. It is called *Koku-Reibo* (*A Bell Ringing in the Empty Sky*). The title refers to the death of Zen monk Fuke-Zenji, who used to walk around ringing a small hand-bell. On his death, the sound of his bell could be heard getting fainter and fainter as it ascended into the clear blue sky. This and other ancient shakuhachi compositions are regarded as sacred and to be played only by great masters.

Playing the shakuhachi takes great skill, requiring an enormous amount of control and subtlety of expression. The musician performing here, Nyogetsu Seldin, has studied the traditional art of the shakuhachi for thirty years. He studied with Kurahashi Yodo Sensei in Kyoto and is now a Grand Master of the instrument.

The music is riveting. It demands all of your attention, because it depends on such minute details. There are only a few notes, but the variety of sounds is amazing. The player uses slides between notes, shadings of color and sound, variations of intensity, and carefully controlled gradations of volume to produce an atmosphere that is truly mystical. Our excerpt ends after only a few minutes, but the entire composition lasts more than 15 minutes. Listen to the excerpt very carefully, and listen to it several times. Each time you will hear something new. The music will capture your imagination in an entirely new way.

MusicNotes

Listening Sketch for
Javanese Gamelan Music
Gangsaran - Bima Kurda - Gangsaran

Duration: 6:21

Student CD Collection: 1, track 2
Complete CD Collection: 1, track 2

GANGSARAN			
Track **2** (2)	**0:00**	Regular rhythms, same note repeated.
	0:26	Music slows down.
BIMA KURDA			
3 (3)	**0:40**	Melody gathers interest, more notes are heard.
	0:55	Rhythm and melody become steady. Long section.
	2:35	Beginning of dialogue.
	2:57	Quiet section. Occasional shouts and laughter.
	4:20	Louder.
	4:36	Music gets faster again.
	5:18	Repeat of dialogue.
GANGSARAN			
4 (4)	**5:32**	Return of music from the opening section.
	6:15	Abrupt ending.

LISTENING GUIDE

Listening Sketch for Mbira Music
Mandarendare **(A Place Full of Energy)**

Duration: 5:32

Student CD Collection: 1, track 5
Complete CD Collection: 1, track 5

*F*or the Shona, a people who make up most of the population of Zimbabwe and extend also into Mozambique, mbira music is mystical music that is used to communicate with the spirits of ancestors and guardians of the tribe. *Mandarendare* ("A place full of energy") is usually played at a dawn ceremony. The performer on this recording, Forward Kwenda, has been involved in keeping alive the musical traditions of the Shona people since he was a young boy. He says, "When I pick up my mbira, I don't know what is going to happen. The music goes by itself. It is so much greater than a human being can understand."

Although it sounds as though more than one person were playing on this piece, there is only one performer. Three distinct layers of sound can be detected: a deep, regular pattern in the bass and two interlocking lines above it. Although there seems at first to be constant repetition, careful listening will reveal slow, but constant, change. The tone quality is unusual; the notes are surrounded with a hiss or buzz that sounds to our ears like a sonic distortion. This hiss, which adds depth and complexity to the sound, is considered an essential element in mbira playing.

MusicNotes

Paul Dukas (1865–1935)
Fanfare from *La Péri*

Date of composition: 1912
Orchestration: 3 trumpets, 4 French
    horns, 3 trombones, tuba
Duration: 2:22

Student CD Collection: 1, track 26
Complete CD Collection: 1, track 26

A 26 (26)	**0:00**	Full group, *f* (loud), homophony
	0:13	New idea, horns; counterpoint from other instruments
	0:23	Second idea moves to trumpets, rounded off by full group, cadence
	0:50	Back to horns, again rounded off by full group, cadence
B 27 (27)	**1:20**	Middle section, quieter *(mf)*, more sustained, smoother
	1:40	Faster rhythm, crescendo to:
A′ 28 (28)	**1:48**	Modified return of opening, *ff*, leading to final cadence with trumpet flourish

MusicNotes

Franz Schubert (1797–1828)
Song for voice and piano,
   Gretchen am Spinnrade
   (*Gretchen at the Spinning Wheel*)

Date of composition: 1814
Text by Johann Wolfgang von Goethe
Tempo: *Nicht zu geschwind* ("Not too fast")
Meter: §
Key: D minor
Duration: 3:37

Student CD Collection: 1, track 29
Complete CD Collection: 1, track 29

---

29 (29) **0:00** | [Spinning wheel starts up—piano]

REFRAIN

0:02
Meine Ruh' ist hin,	My peace is gone,
Mein Herz ist schwer,	My heart is heavy,
Ich finde sie nimmer	And I will never again
Und nimmermehr.	Find peace.

STANZA 1

0:22
Wo ich ihn nicht hab'	Wherever he is not with me
Ist mir das Grab,	Is my grave,
Die ganze Welt	My whole world
Ist mir vergällt.	Is turned to gall.

STANZA 2

[voice gets higher]

0:36
Mein armer Kopf	My poor head
Ist mir verrückt,	Is crazed,
Mein armer Sinn	My poor mind
Ist mir zerstückt.	Is shattered.

REFRAIN

[voice resumes original range]

0:54
Meine Ruh' ist hin,	My peace is gone,
Mein Herz ist schwer,	My heart is heavy,
Ich finde, ich finde sie nimmer	And I will never again
Und nimmermehr.	Find peace.

STANZA 3

1:14
Nach ihm nur schau' ich	I look out the window
Zum Fenster hinaus,	Only to see him,
Nach ihm nur geh' ich	I leave the house
Aus dem Haus.	Only to seek him.

STANZA 4

[change to major key]

30 (30) **1:28**
Sein hoher Gang,	His fine gait,
Sein ed'le Gestalt,	His noble form,
Seines Mundes Lächeln,	The smile of his lips,
Seiner Augen Gewalt,	The power of his eyes,

MUSIC NOTES

STANZA 5

1:41

Und seiner Rede	And the magic flow
Zauberfluss,	Of his words,
Sein Händedruck,	The touch of his hands,
Und ach, sein Kuss!	And oh, his kiss!

[intense, dissonant chords; spinning wheel stops and reluctantly starts up again; return to opening minor key]

REFRAIN

31 (31) **2:08**

Meine Ruh' ist hin,	My peace is gone,
Mein Herz ist schwer,	My heart is heavy,
Ich finde, ich finde sie nimmer	And I will never again
Und nimmermehr.	Find peace.

STANZA 6

2:28

Mein Busen drängt sich	My bosom yearns
Nach ihm hin.	For him.
Ach dürft' ich fassen	Oh, if only I could grasp him
Und halten ihn,	and hold him,

STANZA 7

[voice gets higher]

2:42

Und küssen ihn,	And kiss him
So wie ich wollt',	As I would like,
An seinen Küssen	I would die
Vergehen sollt!	From his kisses!

2:55 [repeat of Stanza 7, slightly modified, ending with climactic high notes]

REFRAIN

[partial]

3:16

Meine Ruh' ist hin,	My peace is gone,
Mein Herz ist schwer.	My heart is heavy.

MUSIC NOTES

Wolfgang Amadeus Mozart (1756–1791)
Minuet and Trio from Symphony No. 18
   in F Major, K. 130

Date of composition: 1772

Orchestration: 2 flutes, 4 horns,
    Violins I and II (*this means the two
    groups of violins in the orchestra*),
    violas, cellos, double basses

Meter: $\frac{3}{4}$

Key: F Major

Duration: 2:05

Student CD Collection: 1, track 32

Complete CD Collection: 1, track 32

Listening Guide 1

MINUET		
A 32 (32) **0:00**	First section of minuet. Begins with a graceful melody played softly by the strings; flutes and horns join in for loud ending.
A **0:09**	Repeat of the first section of the minuet.
B **0:18**	The second section of the minuet. Full orchestra, continuing loud.
B **0:27**	Repeat of the second section.

TRIO		
C 33 (33) **0:37**	First section of trio. Contrast of rhythm and texture, soft strings; answered by loud phrase including the flutes.
C **0:51**	Repeat.
D **1:04**	Second section of trio. Whole orchestra, loud; answered by a quiet phrase that gets louder at the end.
D **1:17**	Repeat.

MINUET		
	[The minuet is played again, exactly as before.]
A 34 (34) **1:29**	First section.
A **1:38**	Repeat.
B **1:47**	Second section.
B **1:56**	Repeat.

Listening Guide 2

MINUET		
A 32 (32) **0:00**	First section. (Try tapping.)
A **0:09**	Repeat.
B **0:18**	Second section. (Keep going).
B **0:27**	Repeat.

MusicNotes

TRIO			
C 33 (33)	**0:37**	First section. (The *notes* are longer here, but the tempo and the meter stay exactly the same).
C	**0:51**	Repeat.
D	**1:04**	Second section.
D	**1:17**	Repeat.

MINUET		[whole minuet repeated]	
A 34 (34)	**1:29**	First section.
A	**1:38**	Repeat.
B	**1:47**	Second section.
B	**1:56**	Repeat.

Listening Guide 3

MINUET			
A 32 (32)	**0:00**	First section. Begins in F Major, ends in C Major.
A	**0:09**	Repeat.
B	**0:18**	Second section. Returns to F Major, ends in F.
B	**0:27**	Repeat.

TRIO			
C 33 (33)	**0:37**	First section. Begins in C Major, ends in G Major.
C	**0:51**	Repeat.
D	**1:04**	Second section. Starts in G Major, returns to C.
D	**1:17**	Repeat.

MINUET		[whole minuet repeated]	
A 34 (34)	**1:29**	First section. F, moves to C.
A	**1:38**	Repeat.
B	**1:47**	Second section. Returns to F and ends in F.
B	**1:56**	Repeat.

MusicNotes

Benny Harris (1919–1975)
Crazeology

Date of composition: 1947 (recorded 1994)
Performers: Daniel Ian Smith (tenor saxophone)
 and Mark Poniatowski (bass)
Tempo: Fast
Meter: $\frac{4}{4}$
Key: B-flat
Duration: 5:17

Student CD Collection: 1, track 35
Complete CD Collection: 1, track 35

CHORUS 1		
A 35 (35) **0:00**	Unison; elaborate syncopated phrases
A **0:10**	Unison; repeat
B **0:21**	Unison; shorter leaping phrases; more key changes
A **0:31**	Unison; repeat of A

CHORUS 2		
A 36 (36) **0:40**	Melody and accompaniment (song texture); swinging rhythm and
A **0:51**	free-flowing improvisation
B **1:01**	
A **1:11**	

CHORUS 3		
A **1:21**	Continuation...
A **1:31**	
B **1:41**	
A **1:51**	

CHORUS 4		
A 37 (37) **2:02**	Bass solo; improvisation with snatches of opening melody
A **2:11**	
B **2:21**	
A **2:32**	

CHORUS 5		
A 38 (38) **2:41**	Continuation, with slides, chords, and twangs...
A **2:50**	
B **3:00**	
A **3:11**	

CHORUS 6		
A 39 (39) **3:19**	Sax answered by bass ("call and response"), four measures each
A **3:28**	
B **3:38**	
A **3:47**	

MusicNotes

C H O R U S 7		
A	**3:57**	Continuation (progressively more elaborate)
A	**4:07**	
B	**4:16**	
A	**4:26**	

C H O R U S 8		[r e p e a t o f C h o r u s 1]
A 40 (40) **4:36**		Unison
A	**4:46**	Unison
B	**4:56**	Unison; shorter phrases
A	**5:06**	Unison

MUSICNOTES

**Maddalena Casulana (c. 1540–
  c. 1590)**
**Madrigal, *Morte, te chiamo*
  (*Death, I Call on You*)**

Date of composition: 1570
Small choir
Tempo: Slow
Meter: $\frac{4}{4}$
Duration: 1:38

Student CD Collection: 1, track 41
Complete CD Collection: 1, track 41

41 (41)	**0:00**		*Morte, te chiamo.*	Death, I call on you.
			[one voice enters at a time]	
			"Che voi? Ecco m'appreso."	"What do you want? Here I am."
			[all together; change of harmony]	
	0:21		*Prendi m'e fa che manchi il mio dolore.*	Take me, and make an end to my grief.
			[voices move lower]	
			"Non posso."	"I cannot."
	0:34		*Non poi? Perchè?*	You cannot? Why not?
			[quick dialogue]	
			"Perch'in te non regna il core."	"Because your heart no longer reigns in your body"
			[more homophonic]	
	0:43		*Sì fa!*	Do it!
			"Non fa!"	"I shall not!"
			[alternating duets]	
			Fatte'l' restituire,	Then give me back my heart,
			[cadence]	
	0:52		*Chè chi vita non ha non può morire.*	For a person who has no life cannot die.
			[smoother homophony]	
	1:03		[last four lines repeated]	

MusicNotes

Kyrie (plainchant)

Men's choir
Duration: 2:06

Student CD Collection: 1, track 42
Complete CD Collection: 1, track 42

*T*his is a chant from a medieval Roman Catholic Mass. It is one of many settings of this text. Although most of the Mass was in Latin, the words to the Kyrie are in Greek. There are three statements in the text: "Kyrie eleison—Christe eleison—Kyrie eleison" ("Lord, have mercy—Christ, have mercy—Lord, have mercy"). And each of these three statements is sung three times. There is great symbolism in this repetition scheme: the number three represented the Trinity, and three times three was considered absolute perfection.

Corresponding to the three statements of the text, there are three phrases of music. The whole piece begins and ends on G, so it is in the G mode, Mixolydian. As in painting, however, a composition may have a mixture of colors, and there are hints of the Phrygian mode in the first phrase, which ends on E. The shape of the melody is very carefully designed. The first phrase is the shortest and moves in waves. The second phrase starts high, and the motion is mostly descending. The last phrase is in the form of an arch and starts and ends on the same note (G). At the top of the arch, the music reaches up to the highest note in the whole piece. The last time the third statement of the text is sung, the music changes slightly, with the addition of three notes to the beginning of the phrase.

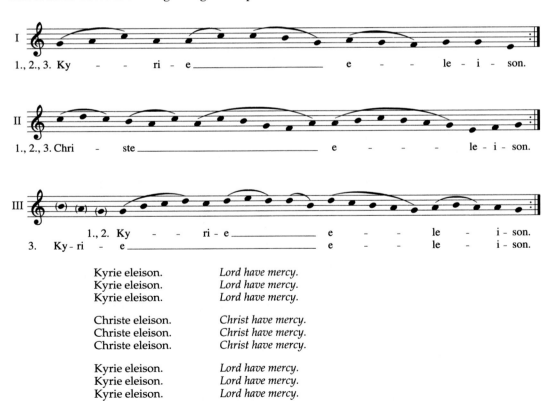

Kyrie eleison.	*Lord have mercy.*
Kyrie eleison.	*Lord have mercy.*
Kyrie eleison.	*Lord have mercy.*
Christe eleison.	*Christ have mercy.*
Christe eleison.	*Christ have mercy.*
Christe eleison.	*Christ have mercy.*
Kyrie eleison.	*Lord have mercy.*
Kyrie eleison.	*Lord have mercy.*
Kyrie eleison.	*Lord have mercy.*

MUSIC NOTES

Beatriz de Dia (late twelfth century)
Song, *A chantar*

Date of composition: c. 1175
Duration: 5:21

Student CD Collection: 1, track 43
Complete CD Collection: 1, track 43

43 (43)   **0:00** | [vielle prelude]

STANZA 1

[vielle accompaniment]

0:25

A chantar m'er de so q'ieu no voldria,	I must sing, whether I want to or not.
Tant me rancur de lui cui sui amia,	I feel so much pain from him whose friend I am,
Car eu l'am mais que nuilla ren que sia;	For I love him more than anything.
Vas lui nom val merces ni cortesia,	But neither grace nor courtesy has any effect on him,
Ni ma beltatz, ni mos pretz, ni mos sens.	Nor my beauty, my decency, or my intelligence.
C'atressim sui enganad'e trahia	I am despised and betrayed,
Cum degr'esser, s'ieu fos desavinens.	As though I were worthless.

1:50   [flute interlude]

STANZA 5

[vielle accompaniment]

3:01

Valer mi deu mos pretz e mos paratges	My decency and my ancestry have their value,
E ma beutatz e plus mos fis coratges,	As do my beauty and the depth of my heart.
Per q'ieu vos mand lai on es vostr'estatges	So I send to your noble home
Esta chansson que me sia messatges:	This song: let it be my messenger!
E voill saber, lo mieus bels amics gens,	And I want to know, my fair friend,
Per que vos m'etz tant fers ni tant salvatges,	Why you are so savage and cruel to me.
Non sal si s'es orguoills o mals talens.	I don't know: is it pride or ill will?

TORNADA

[lute and drum join in softly]

4:18

Mas aitan plus vuoill li digas, messatges,	But I want even more for you to tell him, messenger,
Q'en trop d'orguoill ant gran dan maintas gens.	That pride has been the downfall of many people!

5:01   [florid ending]

MusicNotes

Perotinus (c.1170–c.1236)
***Viderunt Omnes* (four-voice polyphony**
   for the Cathedral of Notre Dame)

Date of composition: 1199
Solo singers and choir
Duration: 4:42

Student CD Collection: 1, track 44
Complete CD Collection: 1, track 44

POLYPHONY					
44 (44)	**0:00**	(soloists)	*Vi-* (sustained-tone)	[rhythmic upper voices throughout]	
	0:57	(soloists)	*de-* (sustained-tone)		
	1:25	(soloists)	*runt* (sustained-tone)	[dissonant opening; brief cadence for end of word]	
	2:29	(soloists)	*om-* (rhythmic/sustained-tone)		
	3:40	(soloists)	*nes* (sustained-tone)	[strong dissonance just before cadence]	
		[cadence]			

MONOPHONY					
45 (45)	**3:46**	(choir)	*fines terrae salutare Dei nostri. Jubilate Deo omnis terra.*	[smooth plainchant]	
		[cadence]			

Viderunt omnes fines terrae salutare Dei nostri. Jubilate Deo omnis terra.

All the ends of the earth have seen the salvation of our God. Praise God all the earth.

MUSIC NOTES

Guillaume de Machaut (c. 1300–1377)
Secular song (rondeau)
Doulz Viaire Gracieus

Date of composition: Mid-fourteenth century
Voice, lute, and recorder
Duration: 2:00

Student CD Collection: 1, track 46
Complete CD Collection: 1, track 46

46 (46)	0:00	*Doulz viaire gracieus,*	*Sweet, gracious countenance,*
	0:12	*De fin cuer vous ay servy.*	*I have served you with a faithful heart.*
	0:30	Weillies moy estre piteus,	Take pity on me,
	0:42	*Doulz viaire gracieus;*	*Sweet, gracious countenance;*
	0:55	Se je sui un po honteus,	If I am a little shy,
	1:07	Ne me mettes en oubli.	Do not forget me.
	1:25	*Doulz viaire gracieus,*	*Sweet, gracious countenance,*
	1:38	*De fin cuer vous ay servy.*	*I have served you with a faithful heart.*

LISTENING GUIDE

Thomas Aquinas (1225–1274)
Plainchant hymn, *Pange Lingua*

Date of composition: Thirteenth century
Choir
Duration: 2:24

Student CD Collection: 1, track 47
Complete CD Collection: 1, track 47

47 (47)	0:00	Stanza 1	(*"Pange lingua …"*)
	0:33	Stanza 2	(*"Nobis datus …"*)
	1:04	Stanza 3	(*"In supremae …"*)
	1:39	Stanza 4	(*"Verbum caro …"*)
	2:12	"Amen"	

MUSICNOTES

Josquin Desprez (c. 1440–1521)
Kyrie from the *Pange Lingua* Mass

Date of composition: c. 1520
Sopranos, altos, tenors, basses
Duration: 2:51

Student CD Collection: 1, track 48
Complete CD Collection: 1, track 48

48 (48)	**0:00**	*Kyrie eleison*	(Based on opening of hymn melody.) Tenors and basses; cadence overlaps with entry of altos. Sopranos enter before final cadence.
	0:45	*Christe eleison*	(Based on lines 3 and 4 of hymn melody.) Paired imitation, overlapping entries.
	2:02	*Kyrie eleison*	(Based on lines 5 and 6 of hymn melody.) Sopranos, altos, tenors, basses enter in turn; increase in activity before final cadence.

MUSIC NOTES

Giovanni Pierluigi da Palestrina
   (c. 1525–1594)
Motet, *Exsultate Deo*

Date of composition: 1584
Sopranos, altos I, altos II, tenors, basses
Duration: 2:24

Student CD Collection: 1, track 49
Complete CD Collection: 1, track 49

49 (49)	**0:00**	*Exsultate Deo adiutori nostro,*	Sing out in praise of God our refuge,	[Imitation in pair of upper voices alone; rising line on "Exsultate."]
	0:11			[Pair of lower voices. Cadence in all five voices; overlaps with:]
	0:28	*iubilate Deo Iacob.*	acclaim the God of Jacob.	[Many entries, suggesting a crowd "acclaiming."]
	0:37			[Lower voices.]
	0:49	*Sumite psalmum et date tympanum,*	Raise a melody; beat the drum,	[Quite homophonic, becoming more imitative. Note dotted rhythm on "tympanum."]
	1:04	*psalterium iucundum cum cithara.*	play the tuneful lyre and harp.	[Elaborate flowering of the voices on "iucundum" ("tuneful").]
50 (50)	**0:00**	*Buccinate in neomenia tuba,*	Blow the trumpet at the new moon,	[Multiple echoes on "Buccinate;" homophonic climax on "neomenia"]
	0:13			[Running echoes on "tuba."]
	0:23	*insigni die solemnitatis vestrae.*	and blow it at the full moon on the day of your solemn feast.	[Slower, lower, more "solemn."]

MUSICNOTES

Thomas Morley (1557–1602)
Two English Madrigals

Date of composition: 1595
Two sopranos (*Sweet Nymph Come to Thy Lover*); two baritones (*Fire and Lightning*)
Duration: 2:31

Student CD Collection: 1, track 51
Complete CD Collection: 1, track 51

51 (51)	**0:00**	Sweet nymph come to thy lover,	Imitation.
	0:12	Lo here alone our loves we may discover,	Touches of homophony on "Lo here alone."
	0:20	(*Repeat of first two lines*)	
	0:39	Where the sweet nightingale with wanton gloses,	Imitation; high notes and close harmony on "gloses" [trills].
	0:49	Hark, her love too discloses.	High notes, very close imitation, especially last time through.
	1:03	(*Repeat of last two lines*)	
52 (52)	**0:00**	Fire and lightning from heaven fall	Lively; very close imitation.
	0:08	And sweetly enflame that heart with love arightful,	Smooth descending scales on "sweetly."
	0:16	(*Repeat of first two lines*)	
	0:31	Of Flora my delightful,	Scales in opposite direction on "delightful."
	0:45	So fair but yet so spiteful.	Last time through: homophonic, close pungent harmony, dissonance on "spite-," incomplete sound on "ful."
	0:47	(*Repeat of last two lines*)	

MUSICNOTES

Giovanni Gabrieli (c. 1555–1612)
Canzona Duodecimi Toni

Date of composition: 1597
Two brass choirs
Duration: 3:53

Student CD Collection: 1, track 53
Complete CD Collection: 1, track 53

INTRO		
53 (53)	0:00	Fairly slow, medium loud, both brass choirs; canzona rhythm is prominent.

SECTION 1		
54 (54)	0:15	Faster tempo, same musical motive and rhythm, faster tempo, homophonic, Choir I.
	0:20	Choir II, growing louder.
	0:27	Both choirs, loud, featuring flourishes by trumpets in imitation; cadence.

SECTION 2		
55 (55)	0:43	Second motive, quieter, mostly homophonic, echoes, passages of imitation between choirs, lively rhythms; cadence.

SECTION 3		
56 (56)	1:26	Third motive, loud, mostly homophonic, echoes, both choirs.
	1:43	Trumpet flourishes, cadence.
	1:49	Canzona rhythm; close imitation, cadence.

SECTION 4		
57 (57)	2:10	Fourth motive, quiet, canzona rhythm, lots of imitation between choirs, cadence.
	2:35	Multiple echoes, from loud to soft, between choirs; crescendo ...
	3:02	Final motive, both choirs loud, leading to big climax.

MUSICNOTES

Claudio Monteverdi (1567–1643)
Orfeo's recitative, Euridice's recitative,
   chorus of nymphs and shepherds,
   and instrumental ritornello
from the opera *Orfeo*

Date of composition: 1607
Tenor and soprano solo, chorus,
   instrumental ensemble and basso
   continuo
Duration: 3:55

Student CD Collection: 1, track 58
Complete CD Collection: 2, track 1

ORFEO			
		[soft arpeggiated chords in continuo]	
58 (1)	0:00	*Rosa del Ciel, vita del mondo, e degna*	O Rose of Heaven, life of the world,
		Prole di lui che l'Universo affrena,	And worthy offspring of him who rules the universe,
		[voice becoming more animated]	
	0:25	*Sol, ch'il tutto circondi e'l tutto miri*	Sun, you who surround and watch everything
		Da gli stellanti giri,	From the starry skies,
		[rising melody]	
	0:34	*Dimmi, vedesti mai*	Tell me, have you ever seen
		Di me più lieto e fortunato amante?	A happier or more fortunate lover than I?
		[gentle cadence]	
	0:45	*Fu ben felice il giorno,*	Blessed was the day,
		Mio ben, [loving phrase] *che pria ti vidi,*	My love, when first I saw you,
	0:56	*E più felice l'ora*	And more blessed yet the hour
		Che per te sospirai,	When first I sighed for you,
		Poich'al mio sospirar tu sospirasti.	Since you returned my sighs.
		[sighing phrases]	
	1:15	*Felicissimo il punto*	Most blessed of all the moment
		Che la candida mano,	When you offered me your white hand,
		Pegno di pura fede, a me porgesti.	As pledge of your pure love.
		[many notes]	
	1:34	*Se tanti cori avessi*	If I had as many hearts
		Quant'occh'il Ciel eterno, e quante chiome	As the eternal sky has eyes, and as many as these hills
		Han questi colli ameni il verde maggio,	Have leaves in the verdant month of May,
	1:45	[one "full" note]	
		Tutti colmi sarieno e traboccanti	They would all be full and overflowing
		Di quel piacer ch'oggi mi fa contento.	With the joy that now makes me happy.
		[soft cadence]	

MusicNotes

		[soft lute chords]	
59 (2)	2:09	*Io non dirò qual sia*	I shall not say how much
		[happy phrases]	
	2:15	*Nel tuo gioir, Orfeo, la gioia mia,*	I rejoice, Orfeo, in your rejoicing,
	2:21	*Che non ho meco il core,*	For my heart is no longer my own
	2:27	*Ma teco stassi in compagnia d'Amore;*	But stands with you in the company of Love;
		["lui" emphasized]	
	2:35	*Chiedilo dunque a lui, s'intender brami,*	Ask of *it* then, if you wish to know,
	2:42	*Quanto lieto gioisca, e quanto t'ami.*	How much happiness it enjoys, and how much it loves you.
		[soft cadence]	

CHORUS

		[happy imitation, duple meter]	
60 (3)	2:59	*Lasciate i monti,*	Leave the hills,
		Lasciate i fonti,	Leave the streams,
		Ninfe vezzose e liete,	You charming and happy nymphs,
		[same music]	
	3:09	*E in questi prati*	Practiced in dancing,
		Ai balli usati	And in these meadows
		Vago il bel pie rendete.	Move your pretty legs.
		[change of key, homophony, triple meter]	
	3:18	*Qui miri il Sole*	Here the Sun
		Vostre carole	Sees your dances,
		Più vaghe assai di quelle,	More beautiful yet than those
		[same music]	
	3:26	*Ond'a la Luna*	Which the stars dance
		La notte bruna	To the light of the moon
		Danzano in Ciel le stelle.	In dusky night.

INSTRUMENTAL RITORNELLO

	3:33	Faster; recorders, strings, basso continuo

MUSICNOTES

Henry Purcell (1659–1695)
Dido's lament from the opera
Dido and Aeneas

Date of composition: 1689
Voice, strings, and harpsichord
Duration: 4:07

Student CD Collection: 1, track 61
Complete CD Collection: 2, track 4

RECITATIVE			
61 (4)	**0:00**	Thy hand, Belinda, darkness shades me,	[slowly descending voice throughout the recitative]
	0:19	On thy bosom let me rest.	
	0:29	More I would, but Death invades me:	
	0:40	Death is now a welcome guest.	[minor chord on "Death;" dissonance on "welcome guest"]
	0:54	[beginning of ground bass: quiet, slow, descending chromatic line heard throughout aria]	

ARIA			
62 (5)	**1:08** (**1:43**)	When I am laid in earth,	[ground bass pattern begins again on "am"]
	1:20 (**1:55**)	May my wrongs create	[no pause between these two lines]
	1:27	No trouble in thy breast.	[voice falls on the word "trouble"]
	(**2:02**)	[repeat]	
63 (6)	**2:17**	Remember me, but ah! forget my fate.	[much repetition; highly expressive rising lines; last "ah" is particularly lyrical]
	2:42	[several repeats]	
	3:30	[cadences of voice and ground bass coincide]	
64 (7)	**3:32**	[quiet orchestral closing; conclusion of chromatic descent]	
	4:02	[final cadence with trill]	

MusicNotes

Antonio Vivaldi (1678–1741)
First Movement from Violin Concerto,
    Op. 8, No. 1, *La Primavera* ("Spring"),
    from *The Four Seasons*

Date of composition: 1725
Solo violin, strings, and harpsichord
Duration: 3:34

Student CD Collection: 1, track 65
Complete CD Collection: 2, track 12

ALLEGRO		["fast"]		
65 (12)	**0:00**	"Spring has arrived, and full of joy"	[Ritornello in tonic, first half, loud and then soft]
	0:15		[Ritornello in tonic, second half, loud and then soft]
	0:32	"The birds greet it with their happy song."	[Trills; three solo violins alone, no basso continuo]
	1:08		[Ritornello in tonic, second half, once only, loud]
	1:16	"The streams, swept by gentle breezes, Flow along with a sweet murmur."	[Quiet and murmuring]
66 (13)	**1:41**		[Ritornello in dominant, second half, once only, loud]
	1:49	"Covering the sky with a black cloak, Thunder and lightning come to announce the season."	[Fast repeated notes; flashing runs and darting passages]
67 (14)	**2:17**		[Ritornello in C# minor, second half, once only, loud]
	2:25	"When all is quiet again, the little birds Return to their lovely song."	[Long, sustained, single note in bass; rising solo phrases, trills again]
	2:43		[Buildup to:
	3:10		Ritornello in tonic, second half twice, first loud and then soft]

MusicNotes

Johann Sebastian Bach (1685–1750)
St. Matthew Passion (excerpt)

Date of composition: c. 1727
Soprano, tenor, and bass voices,
   chorus, orchestra, and basso
   continuo
Duration: 8:07

Student CD Collection: 2, track 1
Complete CD Collection: 2, track 22

---

1 (22)   **0:00** | [orchestral introduction]

SOPRANO

[aria]

2 (23)   **0:31**

Blute nur, blute nur   Only bleed, only bleed,
Blute nur, du liebes Herz,   Only bleed, you dearest heart.

[repeat text four times; answering phrases on flutes and violins; motion throughout in orchestra]

1:19   [orchestral interlude]

3 (24)   **1:51**   [change of key, similar accompanying figures as A section]

Ach! ein Kind das du erzogen,   Ah! a child that you raised
das an deiner Brust gesogen,   and nursed at your breast
droht den Pfleger zu ermorder,   has become a snake
denn es ist zur Schlange worden;   and bites the one who cared for it;

2:21   [repeat, varied]

3:00   [orchestral passage from beginning]

4 (25)   **3:32**   *Blute nur, du liebes Herz* ... [repeated exactly as beginning]

4:20   [orchestral closing passage]

EVANGELIST

[simple basso continuo accompaniment]

5 (26)   **5:00**

Aber am ersten Tage der   Now on the first day of the feast of
   süssen Brot   unleavened bread
traten die Jünger zu Jesu   the disciples came to Jesus
und sprachen zu ihm: and said to him:

CHORUS

[noble, serious tone]

5:10

Wo, wo, wo willst du, dass wir dir   Where, where, where will you have us
   bereiten, das Osterlamm zu essen?   prepare for you to eat the Passover?
Wo willst du, dass wir dir bereiten das   Where will you have us prepare for you
   Osterlamm zu essen?   to eat the Passover?

EVANGELIST

[recitative]

5:36   *Er sprach:*   He said:

MusicNotes

JESUS

[accompanied recitative—violins form a "halo" around the words of Jesus]

6 (27) **5:39**

Gehet hin in die Stadt zu	Go to the city to a certain
einem und sprecht zu ihm:	man and say to him:
Der Meister lässt dir sagen:	The Master says to you:
Meine Zeit is hier,	My time is here,
ich will bei dir die Ostern halten	I will keep the Passover at your house
mit meinen Jüngern.	with my disciples.

EVANGELIST

[recitative—simple basso continuo accompaniment]

6:08

Und die Jüngern täten, wie	And the disciples did as
ihnen Jesus befohlen hatte,	Jesus had commanded,
und bereiteten das Osterlamm.	and prepared the Passover.
Und am Abend satzte er sich	And at evening he sat at the
zu Tische mit den Zwölfen,	table with the twelve,
Und da sie assen, sprach er:	and as they ate, he said:

JESUS

[accompanied recitative]

6:32

Warlich, ich sage euch:	Truly, I say to you:
Eines unter euch wird mich verraten.	One of you will betray me.

["halo;" dissonance and intensity on "betray"]

EVANGELIST

[recitative]

6:50

Und sie wurden sehr betrübt	And they became very troubled
Und huben an, ein jeglicher	and they spoke, each one
unter ihnen, und sagten zu ihm:	of them, and said to Him:

CHORUS

[fast, panicky music]

7 (28) **6:59**

Herr, bin ichs? bin ichs?	Lord, is it I? Is it I? Is it I? Is it I?
bin ichs? bin ichs?	
Herr, bin ichs? bin ichs?	Lord, is it I? Is it I? Is it I? Is it I?
bin ichs? bin ichs?	
Herr, bin ichs? bin ichs? bin ichs?	Lord, is it I? Is it I? Is it I?

CHORALE

[calm setting of final chorale]

7:11

Ich bins, ich sollte büssen,	I should bear all of it,
an Händen und an Füssen	my hands and feet tethered
gebunden in her Höll;	in the bonds of Hell;
Die Geiseln und die Banden	the scourges and shackles
und was du ausgestanden,	that You endured
das hat verdienet meine Seel'.	so that my soul might be delivered.

MusicNotes

George Frideric Handel (1685–1759)
"Halleluyah" Chorus from *Messiah*

Date of composition: 1741
Chorus and orchestra
Duration: 3:49

Student CD Collection: 2, track 8
Complete CD Collection: 2, track 33

8 (33)	**0:00**		Instrumental opening ("pre-echo").

HOMOPHONIC

[Two phrases, each with five statements of "Halleluyah."
Notice the changing rhythms.]

0:07	First phrase, tonic.
0:16	Second phrase, dominant.

UNISON

[With homophonic "halleluyah" responses: "For the Lord God
omnipotent reigneth."]

0:25	First phrase, dominant.
0:37	Second phrase, tonic.

POLYPHONIC

9 (34)	**0:49**	Statement by sopranos, tonic.
	0:56	Statement by tenors and basses, dominant.
	1:05	Statement by tenors and altos, tonic.
	1:14	Short instrumental interlude.

HOMOPHONIC

[With noticeable change in dynamics: two phrases, one soft
(*piano*), one loud (*forte*).]

1:16	*piano:* "The kingdom of this world is become ..."
1:27	*forte:* "... the kingdom of our God and of His Christ."

IMITATION

[Four entries, "And He shall reign forever and ever."]

10 (35)	**1:38**	Basses, tonic.
	1:43	Tenors in counterpoint with basses, dominant.
	1:49	Altos in counterpoint with basses and tenors, tonic.
	1:55	Sopranos in counterpoint with all other voices, dominant.

UNISON

[Three declamatory statements ("King of Kings and Lord of Lords")
against homophonic responses ("forever and ever, halleluyah, halleluyah"), each at a different pitch, moving higher and higher.]

11 (36)	**2:01**	Sopranos and altos, answered by other voices.

MUSIC NOTES

[Two statements of "And he shall reign forever and ever," against contrapuntal responses ("and he shall reign . . .").]

2:42 Basses, dominant.

2:48 Sopranos, tonic.

[Combination of unison and homophonic textures—"King of Kings" . . . ("forever and ever") "and Lord of Lords" . . . ("halleluyah, halleluyah").]

2:54 Tenors, answered by other voices.

[Statements by all voices.]

3:03 "And He shall reign forever and ever."

3:10 "King of Kings and Lord of Lords" (twice).

3:19 "And he shall reign forever and ever."

[Final statement of "King of Kings and Lord of Lords."]

3:26 Tenors and sopranos, answered by other voices.

3:34 Pause; one final drawn-out homophonic statement: plagal cadence (IV–I).

MUSIC NOTES

Franz Joseph Haydn (1732–1809)
Minuet and Trio from Symphony No. 45
   in F-sharp minor

Date of composition: 1772
Orchestration: 2 oboes, 2 horns, violins
   I and II, viola, cello, double bass
Tempo: *Allegretto* ("Moderately fast")
Meter: ¾
Key of movement: F♯ Major
Duration: 4:53

Student CD Collection: 2, track 12
Complete CD Collection: 2, track 40

M I N U E T			
A	12 (40)	0:00	The first section of the minuet, in F♯ Major. Graceful dancelike character; full of contrasts; syncopation. Ends with quiet linking passage on violins alone.
A		0:14	Repeat of first section of the minuet.
B (+A')	13 (41)	0:30	The second section of the minuet, longer than the first. Dominant key (C♯ Major). Short loud passage, longer quiet syncopated passage on strings alone. Then a crescendo into a restatement (A') of the first section of the minuet (0:49).
B (+A')		1:05	Repeat of entire second section, including its restatement of A.
T R I O			
C	14 (42)	1:41	First section of trio. Rising phrase for horns, graceful answering phrase for violins.
C		1:56	Repeat.
D (+C')	15 (43)	2:11	Second section of trio, longer than the first. Back to tonic key (F♯ Major). Divided into three parts: beginning, with descending phrases in horns; (2:21) oboes replace the horns, sudden shift to F♯ *minor*; (2:33) shortened restatement (C') of the first section of the trio.
D (+C')		2:40	Repeat of entire second section of trio, including its restatement of C.
M I N U E T			
			[The entire minuet is repeated exactly.]
A	16 (44)	3:10	A section.
A		3:24	Repeat of A section.
B (+A')		3:39	B section, including restatement of A.
B (+A')		4:14	Repeat of B section with restatement of A.

MUSIC NOTES

Franz Joseph Haydn (1732–1809)
Fourth Movement from String Quartet,
  Op. 33, No. 2, in E-flat Major

Tempo: *Presto* ("Very fast")
Meter: $\begin{smallmatrix}6\\8\end{smallmatrix}$
Key: E♭ Major
Duration: 3:08

Student CD Collection: 2, track 17
Complete CD Collection: 2, track 45

A 17 (45) **0:00**	Main theme.
0:06	Repeat.
B **0:12**	First episode.
A **0:28**	Main theme.
B **0:34**	Repeat of first episode.
A **0:50**	Main theme.
C 18 (46) **0:57**	Second episode, many key changes.
A **1:25**	Main theme.
B **1:31**	First episode again.
A **1:48**	Main theme.
D **1:54**	Third episode.
2:13	Pace slows down, anticipation, then:
A **2:23**	Main theme again.
CODA **2:30**	Final cadence?
19 (47) **2:32**	Sudden change of texture and tempo.

MUSIC NOTES

2:45	Final cadence?
2:46	Main theme, broken up into four separate phrases.
2:58	Ending?
3:01	First phrase of main theme!

MUSICNOTES

Wolfgang Amadeus Mozart
(1756–1791)
First Movement from Symphony No. 40
in G minor, K. 550

Date of composition: 1788
Orchestration: Flute, 2 oboes, 2 clarinets, 2 bassoons, 2 horns, and strings
Tempo: *Allegro molto* ("Very fast")
Meter: ⅔
Key: G minor
Duration: 8:16

Student CD Collection: 2, track 20
Complete CD Collection: 3, track 1

EXPOSITION	
	[timings for the repeat are in parentheses]
20 (1) **0:00**	Opening theme: violins, quiet, G minor; closed by full orchestra, loud.
22 (3) **(2:02)**	

Allegro molto

Violins I & II

| **0:24** | Restatement of opening theme, woodwinds added, beginning modulation to second |
| **(2:27)** | key. |

| **0:34** | Energetic bridge passage, loud, full orchestra, preparing for second key. (Central to |
| **(2:37)** | this passage is a strong rising figure, which appears later in the movement.) |

Violins I & II

| **0:50** | Cadence in new key (B♭–relative major). |
| **(2:53)** | |

| **21** (2) **0:52** | Second theme, also quiet, smooth alternation of strings and woodwinds, quite |
| **(2:56)** | chromatic. |

Violins   Clarinets   Violins

MusicNotes

1:10 **(3:14)**		Odd surprise notes.
1:20 **(3:23)**		Cadence.
1:27 **(3:31)**		Spinning-out section (clarinet, bassoon, strings).
1:47 **(3:50)**		Ending passage, loud, whole orchestra.
2:00 **(4:04)**		Final cadences of exposition.
22 (3)	**2:02**	(Exact repetition of entire exposition.)

DEVELOPMENT

23 (4)	**4:09**	Many key changes, by means of first theme dropping down.
	4:23	A "blender" passage, in which the themes are cut up and tossed around; whole orchestra, loud.
24 (5)	**4:52**	Music gets quiet ... quieter (we are expecting the recapitulation ... but:)
	5:09	Suddenly loud (we've been fooled: no recapitulation here).
	5:19	Another preparation, quiet woodwind descent (watch out: is this real ... ?)

RECAPITULATION

25 (6)	**5:24**	YES! (But notice how Mozart sneaks it in ever so quietly.) All goes normally here, though there are some changes from the exposition.
	5:57	New material, loud, whole orchestra (sounds like it's left over from the development). It uses the rising figure from the opening bridge passage (shown above at 0:34).
	6:29	Back on track ...
26 (7)	**6:40**	Second theme: quiet, winds and strings, this time in tonic key (G minor).
	6:58	Surprise notes.
	7:05	New material.

MusicNotes

7:14	Back on track ...
7:21	Spinning out.
7:44	Music opens out to:

CODA

27 (8) **7:53**	Confirming tonic key, floating, quiet.
8:03	Repeated definitive cadences, loud.
8:09	Three final chords.

MusicNotes

Ludwig van Beethoven (1770–1827)
Six Easy Variations on a Swiss Tune in F
Major for Piano, WoO 64

Date of composition: 1790
Tempo: *Andante con moto* ("Fairly
   slow but with motion")
Meter: $\frac{4}{4}$
Key: F Major
Duration: 2:47

Student CD Collection: 2, track 28
Complete CD Collection: 3, track 9

THEME	[*Andante con moto*—"Fairly slow but with motion"]
28 (9) **0:00**	The theme is simple and pleasant. Notice how it ends very much as it begins.

VARIATION 1	
0:23	Beethoven introduces triplets (three notes to a beat) in both the right and the left hand.

VARIATION 2	
0:40	The melody is mostly unchanged in the right hand, but the left hand has jerky, marchlike accompanying rhythms.

VARIATION 3	
29 (10) **1:02**	This variation uses the minor key, and Beethoven indicates that it should be played "smoothly and quietly throughout."
1:28	The last part of this variation is repeated.

VARIATION 4	
1:48	Back to the major and loud again. Octaves in the right hand, triplets in the left.

VARIATION 5	
2:04	The fifth variation is mostly in eighth notes with a little syncopation and some small chromatic decorations.

VARIATION 6	
2:26	Dynamic contrasts, sixteenth-note runs, and trills mark the last variation, which ends with a two-measure coda to round off the piece.

MUSIC NOTES

Ludwig van Beethoven (1770–1827)
Symphony No. 5 in C minor

Date of composition: 1807–8
Orchestration: 2 flutes, 2 oboes, 2
    clarinets, 2 horns, 2 trumpets,
    timpani, strings
Duration: 33:06

Student CD Collection: 2, track 30
Complete CD Collection: 3, track 11

FIRST MOVEMENT

Tempo: *Allegro con brio* ("Fast and vigorous")
Meter: 2/4
Key: C minor
Form: Sonata-Allegro
Duration: 7:26

EXPOSITION

30 (11) **0:00**
    (1:25)

First theme

Opening motive is played *ff* by the strings and clarinets in octaves and then
    repeated a step lower.

0:06
(1:31)

Sudden *p*, strings immediately develop opening motive.

0:14
(1:39)

Crescendo and loud chords lead to a high sustained note in the violins.

0:18
(1:44)

Transition

Opening motive, *ff*, played only once by full orchestra.
Sudden *p*, further development of the opening motive by strings.
Strings gradually crescendo and ascend.
Reiterated timpani notes, sudden stop.

0:43
(2:08)

Horn-call motive, *ff*.

MUSIC NOTES

31 (12) **0:46** | *Second theme*
       (2:11)

A contrasting gentle melody, *p*, relative major key (E♭ Major), accompanied by a version of the opening motive in the lower strings.

0:58 | Crescendo and ascent lead to another new melody: a jubilant theme, *ff*, in the
(2:23)   violins, played twice.

Violins

1:15 | Woodwinds and horns rapidly descend, twice; then a cadence in E♭ minor, using
(2:40)   the rhythm of the basic motive. Pause.

32 (13) **1:25** | (Entire exposition is repeated.)

DEVELOPMENT

33 (14) **2:50** | Opening motive in horns, *ff*, in F minor, echoed by strings.
Sudden *p*, basic motive developed by strings and woodwinds.
Another gradual ascent and crescendo, leading to forceful repeated chords.

3:25 | Horn-call motive in violins, *ff*, followed by descending line in low strings, twice.
Pairs of high chords in woodwinds and brass, *ff*, alternating with lower chords in
    strings, *ff*.
Sudden decrease in volume, alternation between single chords, key changes.
Sudden *ff*, horn -call in full orchestra; return to alternation of wind and string
    chords, *pp*, with key changes.
Sudden *ff*, opening motive repeated many times, leading back to recapitulation.

RECAPITULATION

34 (15) **4:08** | *First theme*

Opening motive, *ff*, in tonic (C minor), full orchestra.
Opening motive developed, strings, *p*, joined by slow-moving melody on one oboe.
Oboe unexpectedly interrupts the music with a short, plaintive solo.

MusicNotes

	4:39	*Transition*

Development of opening motive resumes in strings, ***p***.
Gradual crescendo, full orchestra, ***ff***, repeated timpani notes, sudden stop.
Horn-call motive, ***ff***, in horns.

35 (16)	**5:02**	*Second theme*

Contrasting gentle melody, ***p***, in C Major (the *major* of the tonic!), played
    alternately by violins and flutes. (Basic motive accompanies in timpani when
    flutes play.) Gradual buildup to the return of:
Jubilant string theme, ***ff***, in violins, played twice.
Woodwinds and horns rapidly descend, twice, followed by a cadence using the
    rhythm of the opening motive. Then, without pause, into:

CODA

36 (17)	**5:52**	Forceful repeated chords, ***ff***, with pauses.

Horn-call motive in lower strings and bassoons, along with flowing violin melody,
    f, in tonic (C minor).
Descending pattern, violins, leads to:

	6:17	A completely new theme in the strings, rising up the minor scale in four-note

    sequences.

Four-note fragments of the new theme are forcefully alternated between woodwinds
    and strings.
A short passage of fast, loud, repeated notes leads into a return of the opening
    motive, ***ff***, full orchestra.
Suddenly ***pp***; strings and woodwinds develop the motive for a few seconds.
A swift and dramatic return to full orchestra, ending with ***ff*** chords.

SECOND MOVEMENT

Tempo: *Andante con moto* ("Fairly slow but with motion")
Meter: ⅜
Key: A♭ Major
Form: Modified Theme and Variations
Duration: 10:32

MUSIC NOTES

37 (18) **0:00** | *Theme A*

Lyrical melody in tonic (A♭ Major), first presented by violas and cellos, ***p***.
Accompaniment in basses, pizzicato.

Violas, Cellos

p dolce   *f*   *p*

0:26 | Melody is continued by woodwinds, concludes with alternation between woodwinds
and strings.

38 (19) **0:59** | *Theme B (in two parts)*

(1) A gently rising theme in the clarinets, ***p***, in the tonic.

Clarinets

1:15 | Clarinet theme is taken over by violins, ***pp***.
Sudden crescendo forms a transition to:
(2) A brass fanfare in C Major, ***ff***.
Violins continue this theme, ***pp***. Slow sustained chords and a cadence in the tonic
key form an ending to Theme B.

39 (20) **2:14** | *Variation 1(A)*

Theme A, varied, in the tonic, again on the violas and cellos, ***p***, enhanced by a
smooth, continuously flowing rhythm, and with long notes from the clarinet.

Violas, Cellos

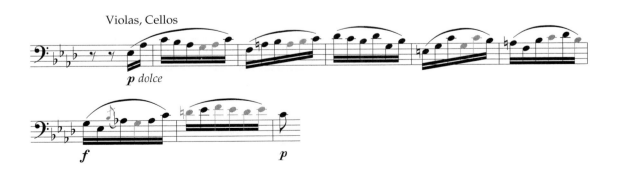

p dolce

f   *p*

MusicNotes

(Note that Variation 1A contains all the notes of the original Theme A. These notes are printed in black in the example above.)
Again, a conclusion with an alternation between the violins and woodwinds.

---

40 (21) **3:05** | *Variation 1(B)*

The B theme—clarinet part as well as fanfare part—is presented with a more active accompaniment.
The concluding sustained chords, **_pp_**, are now accompanied by quick repeated notes in the cellos, and ended by a brighter cadence.

---

41 (22) **4:11** | *Variation 2(A)*

Theme A, varied, again enhanced by a smooth, flowing rhythm, but twice as fast as the first variation, and with long notes from the woodwinds.
This embellished melody is repeated by the violins, **_pp_**, in a higher register.

4:47 | Then the embellished melody is played by the cellos and basses, accompanied by powerful repeated chords. The variation ends on two rising scales, leading to a high sustained note.

---

42 (23) **5:12** | *Central Section*

Sudden **_pp_**, repeated string chords accompany a short, delicate phrase based on Theme A and played by the clarinet, bassoon, and flute in turn. This blossoms into a woodwind interlude, leading to a return of:

6:12 | Brass fanfare from Theme B, **_ff_**, with timpani rolls, in C Major.
A short repeated motive in the strings, **_pp_**, leads to:
Staccato passage in the woodwinds based on Theme A,
but in A♭ *minor.*
Ascending scales in the flute and strings, crescendo, into:

---

43 (24) **7:43** | *Variation 3(A)*

Climactic restatement of melody from Theme A by the full orchestra, **_ff_**. (Violins play melody, while woodwinds work in imitation with violins.)
The end of the first section of the melody is accompanied by rising scales in the strings and woodwinds.
Once more, a conclusion with an alternation between the violins and the flute.

MusicNotes

44 (25)   **8:36**   Faster tempo, single bassoon, **p**, plays a passage based on the beginning of Theme
A, with comments from a single oboe.
Rising melody in the strings, crescendo.

9:04   The original tempo resumes. Flute and strings, **p**, again play the last section of
Theme A, but the violins poignantly extend the final phrase. Cadence in tonic.

9:43   Another variation of the first phrase from Theme A, clarinets, **p**.
First three notes of Theme B (fanfare part), played repeatedly in the low strings,
outlining the tonic chord. Gradually builds in intensity and leads to a cadence
by the full orchestra, **ff**.

Tempo: *Allegro* ("Fast")
Meter: ¾
Key: C minor
Form: Scherzo and Trio, with Transition
Duration: 5:34

[with several internal repetitions of phrases, but no overall
repeats]

45 (26)   **0:00**   Short rising unison melody in cellos and basses, unaccompanied, **pp**, in the tonic
(C minor).

Cellos, Basses

Strings and woodwinds conclude the phrase. Pause.

0:08   Cellos and basses repeat and extend their melody.
Same concluding phrase in the woodwinds and strings.

MusicNotes

| | 0:19 | Sudden *ff*, horns state a powerful repeated-note melody based on the opening short-short-short-LONG pattern from the first movement. |

Horns

| | | This repeated-note melody is developed by the strings and winds, changing key, *f*. |

| **46** (27) | 0:37 | The first melody is restated by the cellos and basses and answered by strings and woodwinds. Pause.
This is resumed and developed. It intensifies, changing keys rapidly, and leads to: |

| | 0:59 | The repeated-note melody in the tonic, played by the full orchestra, *f*.
Volume decreases, dialogue between strings and woodwinds, *p*. |

| | 1:29 | A sprightly, graceful theme in the violins, *p*, accompanied by offbeat chords in the woodwinds. |

| | 1:41 | The scherzo concludes with cadence chords in the short-short-short-LONG rhythm. |

TRIO

| **47** (28) | 1:47 | *Trio Section A* |

Scurrying melody, unaccompanied, in the cellos and basses; in C Major, *f*.

Cellos, Basses

| | | This develops in the style of a fugue and quickly comes to a cadence. |

| | 2:01 | *Trio Section A* (exact repeat) |

MUSIC NOTES

48 (29)	**2:16**	*Trio Section B*

After a couple of humorous false starts, the fuguelike theme continues, *f*, accompanied by a syncopated, leaping melody in the woodwinds. As the sound builds, a portion of the "fugue" theme is stated by the full orchestra, leading to a cadence.

	2:42	*Trio Section B* (altered)

The section begins again, but now the music dwindles down from the winds to a pizzicato melody in the cellos and basses, leading to a return of the scherzo.

RETURN OF SCHERZO

49 (30)	**3:11**	The original minor melody returns, *pp*, but the answering phrase is stated by winds alone. Pause.

The repeat of the melody is played by bassoons and pizzicato cellos and is answered by pizzicato strings. Pause.

	3:30	The powerful horn melody appears, eerily and *pp*, on pizzicato strings with occasional wind comments.

Both themes are again combined and developed (the *pp* continues).

The sprightly theme returns, *pp*, and without its former bouncing character.

Cadence chords, *pp*, in the short-short-short-LONG rhythm, end the scherzo but also begin the next surprising passage.

TRANSITION TO LAST MOVEMENT

50 (31)	**4:17**	A low sustained string tone, *ppp*, accompanies ominous repeated notes in the timpani, *pp*.

	4:27	A violin melody, *pp*, based on the opening of the scherzo, is added to this suspenseful moment.

As the melody rises in pitch, it changes from minor to major. There is a rapid crescendo on a sustained chord, leading without pause into the fourth movement.

FOURTH MOVEMENT

Orchestration: 3 trombones, a piccolo, and a contrabassoon are added to the orchestra for this movement.

Tempo: *Allegro* ("Fast")

Meter: ⁴⁄₄

Key: C Major

Form: Sonata

Duration: 11:27

MUSICNOTES

51 (32) **0:00**

(1:54)

Theme 1

Electrifying marchlike melody, full orchestra, **ƒƒ**, with especially prominent trumpets. The first three notes spell out the tonic chord of C Major.

Trumpets

ƒƒ

0:14

(2:06)

The rising staccato notes of the end of the melody are developed at length, with full orchestration, **ƒƒ**.

0:29

(2:21)

A descending scalar melody with off-the-beat accents leads to the transition theme.

52 (33) **0:34**

(2:26)

Transition Theme (Theme 2)

A new, forceful theme, **ƒƒ**, begins in the horns.

Horns

ƒƒ

0:45

(2:38)

Transition Theme is extended by the violins, leading to a quick dialogue between woodwinds, violins, and low strings, and then:

53 (34) **1:00**

(2:52)

Theme 3

A light, bouncing melody in the violins (dominant key, G Major) with the short-short-short-LONG rhythm, incorporating triplets, contrasts of loud and soft, and a countermelody (colored notes in the example) that becomes important in the development section.

MusicNotes

A frantic, **ff**, scalar passage in the strings, and two loud staccato chords, herald the entrance of:

---

54 (35)   **1:25**
     (3:18)

Closing Theme (Theme 4)

Theme 4, heard first in the strings and woodwinds:

Immediate repeat by the full orchestra, **f**, leading to repeated chords by the full orchestra and an ascending motive in the strings, **ff**, and directly into:

---

55 (36)   **(1:54)**

(Repeat of Exposition)

DEVELOPMENT

[w i d e   m i x   o f   k e y s]

56 (37)   **3:48**

A long section concentrating on the recombination of the triplet motives of Theme 3, eventually accompanied by slowly ascending flute scales.

4:00

Theme 3's countermelody is now put in the spotlight, first by the lower strings and contrabassoon, then by the powerful new trombones, then by the strings and trombones in imitation, and finally by the full orchestra.

4:49

A long, gigantic climax leads to a real surprise:
We hear the short-short-short-LONG horn melody of the scherzo, **pp**, but on strings, clarinets, and oboes.
This reminiscence is swept away by a crescendo and the recapitulation.

MUSICNOTES

57 (38)   **5:52** | *Theme 1*

The marchlike melody is again stated in the full orchestra, **ff**. Once again, the staccato notes at the end of the melody are developed at length, and descending scales lead into the Transition Theme.

6:26 | *Transition Theme (Theme 2)*

Theme 2 is stated in the horns and continued at length by the violins, as in the exposition.

6:55 | *Theme 3*

The triplet-dominated Theme 3 is stated essentially the same way as in the exposition, but with a fuller accompaniment and in the tonic key.

7:21 | *Closing Theme (Theme 4)*

Theme 4 is presented but slightly reorchestrated, leading to a long coda.

58 (39)   **7:50** | The coda begins with further development of Theme 3 and its countermelody.

8:13 | After six staccato chords, the winds develop a variant of Theme 2 in imitation, **p**.

8:35 | This is followed by rapid ascending piccolo scales.

8:45 | The variant of Theme 2 returns, this time in the strings, with piccolo trills and scales.
Then, an acceleration in tempo until:

9:12 | A very fast return to the first part of Theme 4 in the violins. The motive gradually climbs higher, as the full orchestra joins in.
There is a crescendo and fragmentation of the theme, leading to:

9:28 | Theme 1, full orchestra, **ff**, but much faster.
It is quickly developed and comes to an extremely long ending passage of incessantly pounded chords, finally coming to rest on the single note C, played **ff** by the full orchestra.

MusicNotes

Franz Schubert (1797–1828)
Song, *Die Forelle* (*The Trout*)

Date of composition: 1817
Voice and piano
Tempo: *Etwas lebhaft* ("Rather lively")
Meter: $\frac{2}{4}$
Key: D♭ Major
Duration: 2:10

Student CD Collection: 2, track 59
Complete CD Collection: 4, track 1

---

59 (1)	**0:00**	Piano introduction based on the rippling figure.

STANZA 1

[rippling accompaniment continues]

	0:08	*In einem Bächlein helle,*	In a limpid brook
		Da schoss in froher Eil'	In joyous haste
		Die launische Forelle	The whimsical trout
		Vorüber wie ein Pfeil.	Darted about like an arrow.

	0:20	*Ich stand an dem Gestade*	I stood on the bank
		Und sah in süsser Ruh'	In blissful peace, watching
		Des muntern Fischleins Bade	The lively fish swim around
		Im klaren Bächlein zu.	In the clear brook.

[last two lines repeated]

	0:39	Piano interlude

STANZA 2

[same music]

60 (2)	**0:45**	*Ein Fischer mit der Rute*	An angler with his rod
		Wohl an dem Ufer stand,	Stood on the bank,
		Und sah's mit kaltem Blute,	Cold-bloodedly watching
		Wie sich das Fischlein wand.	The fish's flicker.

	0:57	*So lang' dem Wasser Helle,*	As long as the water is clear,
		So dacht' ich, nicht gebricht,	I thought, and not disturbed,
		So fängt er die Forelle	He'll never catch that trout
		Mit seiner Angel nicht.	With his rod.

[last two lines repeated]

	1:17	Piano interlude

MUSICNOTES

[sudden change of rhythm, harmony, and accompanying figures]

61 (3)   **1:23**

Doch endlich ward dem Diebe	But in the end the thief
Die Zeit zu lang. Er macht	Grew impatient. Cunningly
Das Bächlein tückisch trübe,	He made the brook
	cloudy, [diminished sevenths]
Und eh ich es gedacht,	And in an instant [suspense gaps
	in piano]

1:37

So zuckte seine Rute,	His rod quivered,
Das Fischlein zappelt dran,	And the fish struggled on it. [crescendo]
Und ich mit regem Blute	And I, my blood boiling, [earlier music
	returns]
Sah die Betrog'ne an.	Looked at the poor tricked creature.

[last two lines repeated]

1:58   Piano postlude

MUSIC NOTES

Franz Schubert (1797–1828)
Fourth Movement from Quintet in A
Major, D. 667 (*The Trout*)

Date of composition: 1819
Orchestration: Violin, viola, cello,
    double bass, piano
Tempo: *Andantino—Allegretto*
    ("Medium slow"—"A little faster")
Meter $\frac{2}{4}$
Key: D Major
Duration: 8:34

Student CD Collection: 2, track 62
Complete CD Collection: 4, track 4

THEME

| | | Strings only. |

| **62** (4) | **0:00** | First section. |

| | **0:21** | Repeat. |

| | **0:43** | Second section. |

VARIATION I

In this variation, the theme is played by the piano and is slightly embellished. The strings weave an ornamentation around the melody with fast-moving triplets and trills. Listen here to the *pizzicato* bass.

| **63** (5) | **1:19** | First section. |

| | **1:36** | Repeat. |

| | **1:53** | Second section. |

VARIATION II

Now the main melody is taken over by the viola, above which the violin plays ornaments in triple rhythm. The theme is complemented by short imitative phrases in the piano part.

| **64** (6) | **2:40** | First section. |

| | **2:58** | Repeat. |

| | **3:15** | Second section. |

MUSIC NOTES

This variation is dominated by the piano, which plays an uninterrupted flow of fast notes. The theme is played (rather ploddingly!) by the double bass and progresses steadily along this perpetual motion of the piano part.

65 (7)	**3:40**	First section.
	3:55	Repeat.
	4:10	Second section.

VARIATION IV

This variation bursts out loudly in the minor key, but the initial dramatic chords soon yield to a more playful section in triplets. The second half gradually becomes more and more calm, gently introducing the cello.

66 (8)	**4:33**	First section.
	4:49	Repeat.
	5:06	Second section.

VARIATION V

It is the cello that dominates the fifth variation, which is in B♭ Major but is also tinged with melancholy minor touches. The second section is extended to lead the music back to its home key, D Major.

67 (9)	**5:38**	First section.
	6:00	Repeat.
	6:21	Second section.

VARIATION VI

"A little faster." The music livens up for the final variation, which is marked by the rippling accompaniment that characterizes the original song. Violin and cello trade phrases, and the ripple brings the movement to a peaceful conclusion.

68 (10)	**7:16**	First section. Violin with piano.
	7:27	First section repeated. Cello with strings.
	7:40	Second section. Violin/piano.
	7:58	Second section repeated. Cello/strings, joined by piano for quiet ending.

MusicNotes

Fanny Mendelssohn Hensel
  (1805–1847)
Lied **from** *Songs without Words*, **Op. 8,**
  No. 3

Date of composition: 1840?
Tempo: *Larghetto* ("Fairly slow")
Meter: $\frac{4}{4}$
Key: D Major
Duration: 3:05

Student CD Collection: 2, track 69
Complete CD Collection: 4, track 25

A		
69 (25)	**0:00**	Melody repeats a gently curving motive, followed by an ascending leap, as a kind of questioning idea. This is followed by a balanced descending motive. The mood is one of contemplation.
	0:30	Questioning idea in low range, response in higher range.
B		
70 (26)	**1:03**	Modulating, unstable B section—shorter, faster exchanges of questioning idea, answered by descending arpeggios.
	1:20	Minor version of questioning idea in low range. Crescendo, then decrescendo, leads to:
A'		
71 (27)	**1:39**	Clear return of the beginning, moving quickly to faster sequential phrases.
	2:15	Closing section using questioning idea, including crescendo and leap to highest note of the piece. Ends with gentle decrescendo.

MusicNotes

Fryderyk Chopin (1810–1849)
Prelude in E minor, Op. 28, for Piano

Date of composition: 1836–39
Tempo: *Largo* ("Broad")
Meter: $\frac{2}{2}$
Duration: 2:27

Student CD Collection: 3, track 1
Complete CD Collection: 4, track 28

A SECTION		
1 (28) **0:00**	Opening melody. Focus is on descending left-hand accompanying chords. Upper neighbor tone is heard several times in right hand.
0:20	New note, melodic motion continues to descend.
B SECTION		
2 (29) **0:46**	More motion in melody and change in accompanying figures.
1:01	End of section, little flourish in melody, returning to:
A' SECTION		
3 (30) **1:07**	Variation of A.
1:22	More rhythmic activity in both hands.
1:25	Loudest section.
1:35	Feeling of stasis.
1:48	"Goal" reached.
2:01	Final chord?
2:04	Expressive silence.
2:09	Real final cadence (three chords).

MUSICNOTES

Robert Schumann (1810–1856)
Träumerei (Dreaming), from
   Kinderszenen, Op. 15, for Piano

Date of composition:1838
Meter: $\frac{3}{4}$
Key: F Major
Duration: 3:00

Student CD Collection: 3, track 4
Complete CD Collection: 4, track 35

A SECTION

4 (35)   **0:00** | Melody is presented: first phrase:

0:08 | High point of the first phrase.

0:19 | Ending of the first phrase overlaps with the beginning of the second.

0:27 | Melody reaches even higher, to its highest pitch.

0:38 | Cadence.

0:42 | A section repeated.

B SECTION

5 (36)   **1:23** | Melody is presented, but varied melodically and harmonically.

A' SECTION

6 (37)   **2:03** | Melody is restated.

2:31 | Large, rolled chord under the highest pitch of melody ("signal" that the piece will end soon).

2:45 | Ending cadence.

MUSIC NOTES

Franz Liszt (1811–1886)
***Transcendental Étude* No. 10 in F minor**

Date of composition: 1839
Tempo: *Allegro agitato molto*
  ("Fast and very agitated")
Meter: $\frac{2}{4}$
Duration: 4:06

Student CD Collection: 3, track 7
Complete CD Collection: 4, track 40

7 (40)	**0:00**	Starts quietly with fast descending runs.
	0:07	Crescendo, then quiet.
	0:14	Loud and wild.
	0:23	Descending runs again.
8 (41)	**0:26**	Surging melody in octaves in right hand, hectic passagework in left hand.
	0:53	Agitated alternation of short phrases.
	1:07	Heavy chordal melody in bass, fireworks in right hand.
	1:18	Suddenly quiet, surging melody again, crescendo.
9 (42)	**1:32**	Descending runs again.
	1:39	Slow down, quieter.
	1:41	Crescendo and speed up.
10 (43)	**1:51**	Surging melody again, crescendo.
	2:03	Moment of tenderness.
	2:18	Huge crescendo, massive climax.
	2:58	Alternating short phrases again.

MusicNotes

3:12	Heavy bass chords again.
3:29	Contrary motion; stop.
3:33	Coda. Speed up; alternation of very high and very low.
3:55	Massive ending chords.

MusicNotes

Giuseppe Verdi (1813–1901)
Otello (Excerpt)

Date of composition: 1887
Duration: 6:17

Student CD Collection: 3, track 11
Complete CD Collection: 5, track 1

---

11 (1)   **0:00** | [horn, single note]

IAGO

0:04 |
Era la notte, Cassio dormia,
gli stavo accanto.
Con interrotte voci tradia
l'intimo incanto.
Le labbra lente, lente movea,
nell'abbandono del sogno ardente;

I watched Cassio the other night
as he slept.
All of a sudden he began to mutter
what he was dreaming.
Moving his lips slowly, very slowly,
I heard him betray his secret thoughts;

0:40 | *e allor dicea, con flebil suono:*

saying in a passionate voice:

0:48 |
"Desdemona soave!
Il nostro amor s'asconda,
cauti vegliamo

"My sweetest Desdemona!
let us be careful,
cautiously hiding our love,

1:02 | *l'estasi del ciel tutto m'innonda!"*

our heavenly rapture!"

1:14 | [more agitated orchestral accompaniment]

1:16 |
Seguia più vago l'incubo blando;
con molle angoscia l'interna imago
quasi baciando,

Then he moved toward me
and gently caressing
the person in his dreams,

1:32 |
ei disse poscia: "Il rio destino
impreco che al Moro ti donò!"

he said this: "Oh accursed fortune
that gave you to the Moor!"

1:55 |
E allora il sogno
in cieco letargo si mutò.

And after his dream,
he went calmly back to sleep.

OTELLO

12 (2)   **2:17** | *Oh, mostruosa colpa!*

Oh, monstrous deed!

IAGO

Io non narrai che un sogno...

No, this was only his dreaming...

MUSIC NOTES

OTELLO

2:22 | *Un sogno che rivela un fatto…* | A dream that reveals the truth…

IAGO

2:25 | *Un sogno che può dar forma* / *di prova ad altro indizio.* | A dream that may support other evidence.

OTELLO

E qual? | What kind of evidence?

[a little slower; horn note]

IAGO

2:37 | *Talor vedeste* / *in mano di Desdemona* / *un tessuto trapunto a fior* / *e più sottil d'un velo?* | Have you ever seen / in Desdemona's hand / a handkerchief decorated with flowers / and of the finest texture?

OTELLO

2:54 | *È il fazzoletto ch'io le diedi,* / *pegno primo d'amor.* | That is the handkerchief I gave her, / It was my first gift to her.

IAGO

3:01 | *Quel fazzoletto ieri certo ne son* / *lo vidi in man di Cassio.* | That same handkerchief I swear / I saw in Cassio's hand.

OTELLO

[agitated; furious]

13 (3) 3:13 | *Ah! mille gli* / *donasse Iddio!* / *Una è povera preda al furor mio!* / *Iago, ho il cuore di gelo.* / *Lungi da me le pietose larve:* / *Tutto il mio vano amor,* / *esalo al cielo—* / *Guardami, ei sparve!* / *Nelle sue spire d'angue l'idra m'avvince!* | Ah! May God give the slave / a thousand lives! / One is all too little for my revenge! / Iago, my heart is ice. / Rise, Vengeance, from your cave: / my deepest love— / I vow to heaven— / look, it's gone! / I yield to tyrannous hate!

3:49 | *Ah sangue! sangue! sangue!* | Oh blood! blood! blood!

MusicNotes

	[determined]	
3:56	*Si pel ciel marmoreo giuro!* *Per le attorte folgori,* *per la Morte e per l'oscuro mar* *sterminator.* *D'ira e d'impeto tremendo,* *presto fia che sfolgori questa man* *ch'io levo e stendo!*	I swear by yonder marble heaven! and the eternal stars above, and the darkest sea below, Never shall my anger cease until this hand has brought about my revenge!

IAGO

4:28	*Non v'alzate ancor!* *Testimon è il Sol ch'io miro;* *che m'irradia e inanima,* *l'ampia terra e il vasto spiro,* *del Creato inter;* *che ad Otello io sacro ardenti,* *core, braccio ed anima s'anco* *ad opere cruenti*	No, wait! Witness Sun, which illumines us: Earth, on which we live, you, ambient air that we breathe, the Creator's breath; witness that I eagerly give Othello my heart, my hands, and my soul to these bloody deeds.

5:01	*s'armi suo voler!*	Let him command!

OTELLO & IAGO

		[duet, rising to a powerful climax]	
14 (4)	5:07	*Si pel ciel marmoreo giuro!* *per le attorte folgori,* *per la Morte e per l'oscuro per mar* *sterminator.*	I swear by yonder marble heaven! and eternal stars above, and the darkest sea below,

	5:25	*D'ira e d'impeto tremendo* *presto fia che sfolgori questa man* *ch'io levo e stendo;* *presto fia che sfolgori questa man,* *presto fia che sfolgori questa man*	Never shall my anger cease until this hand has brought about my revenge; until this hand, until this hand

	5:46	*ch'io levo e stendo.*	has brought about my revenge.

	5:53	*Dio vendicator!* [unaccompanied]	God of vengeance!

	5:59	[loud orchestral postlude; brass and timpani; whole orchestra]

	6:13	[End of Act II]

MUSIC NOTES

Johannes Brahms (1833–1897)
Fourth Movement from Symphony No. 4
  in E minor

Date of composition: 1885
Duration: 10:36
Orchestration: 2 flutes, 2 oboes,
    2 clarinets, 2 bassoons,
    contrabassoon, 4 French horns,
    2 trumpets, 3 trombones, timpani,
    full string section
Tempo: *Allegro energico e passionato*
    ("Fast, energetic, and passionate")
Meter: $\frac{3}{4}$
Key: E minor

Student CD Collection: 3, track 15
Complete CD Collection: 5, track 34

A SECTION		

[minor key, 3/4 meter]

15 (34)   **0:00**   Theme. Strong, measure-long chords, ascending melodic line, brass and woodwinds. (Count the eight measures.)

0:16   *Variation 1*

Also chordal, with timpani rolls and string pizzicatos on the second beat of the measures.

0:30   *Variation 2*

Smooth melody with regular rhythmic values and smooth motion. Flutes join clarinets and oboes in a crescendo.

0:46   *Variation 3*

The regular rhythm of the melody is given a staccato articulation; brass is added.

MUSIC NOTES

1:01		*Variation 4*
		The ascending melody of the theme is used as a bass line in the lower strings, while the violins introduce a new melody, featuring leaping motion and jumpy rhythms.
1:18		*Variation 5*
		Violins elaborate this melody with faster rhythms; accompaniment thickens with arpeggios.
1:33		*Variation 6*
		Rhythms become even faster and more intense, building to the next variation.
1:48		*Variation 7*
		New melodic idea, with the violins strained in their upper register, and a new jumpy rhythm.
16 (35)	**2:04**	*Variation 8*
		Faster rhythms (sixteenth notes) used in violins, busy energetic feel; violins repeat a single high note while the flute plays a smoother melodic line.
	2:19	*Variation 9*
		Suddenly loud; even faster rhythms (sixteenth-note triplets), violins swoop from high to low range; decrescendo with violins again on repeated note; descending chromatic scale in the winds.
	2:35	*Variation 10*
		Calm exchanges of chords between winds and strings.
	2:53	*Variation 11*
		More chord exchanges, but the violins elaborate theirs with faster, detached notes. Descending and slowing chromatic scale in the flute connects to solo of the next variation.

MUSIC NOTES

[Here the new, slower tempo and meter (3/2) result in longer variations, although they are still eight measures. The descending chromatic scale that ended Variation 11 also ends Variations 13, 14, and 15.]

17 (36)　**3:14** | *Variation 12*

Flute solo that restlessly ascends, gradually reaching into higher ranges, and then descends. Duple pattern in accompaniment emphasizes the new meter.

3:57 | *Variation 13*

Change to brighter E Major. Much calmer mood. Clarinet and oboe alternate simple phrases. Duple pattern in accompaniment continues, supplemented by long rising arpeggios in the strings.

4:36 | *Variation 14*

Trombones enter with chordal, hymnlike sound. Short rising arpeggios in the strings are the only accompaniment.

5:17 | *Variation 15*

Brass and winds continue rich chordal sound, with fuller string arpeggios, as in Var. 14. Descending line in flute, slows to a halt.

A' SECTION

[The return of the A material is bold and dramatic. The faster tempo has renewed drive and energy after the contemplative B section.]

18 (37)　**6:03** | *Variation 16*

Repeat of the original statement of the theme, only joined in measure 4 by searingly high violins descending a scale. Back to E minor and 3/4.

6:16 | *Variation 17*

String tremolos crescendo and decrescendo while winds emphasize beats 2 and 3 of the 3/4 meter.

6:27 | *Variation 18*

String tremolos continue while winds and brass exchange a jumpy figure that builds in a rising melody.

MusicNotes

6:40	*Variation 19*	
	f; new staccato articulation as strings and winds alternate bold eighth-note gestures.	
6:53	*Variation 20*	
	Staccato figure builds in intensity, using faster triplet rhythm.	
7:05	*Variation 21*	
	Swift ascending scales in strings, ending with accented notes, alternate with brass unison attacks rising in pitch.	
7:18	*Variation 22*	
	p; syncopated quarter notes, creating a two-against-three feeling, are exchanged with staccato triplet figures.	
7:30	*Variation 23*	
	Suddenly f; theme in French horns, triplet figures build in strings and winds, ending in eighth notes moving by leaps.	
19 (38) **7:44**	*Variation 24*	
	With its accents on beat 2, this variation recalls Var. 1 but is much more forceful, with heavy accents.	
7:59	*Variation 25*	
	Here the soft melody of Var. 2 returns, now frenzied in intensity through the loud volume and string tremolos. Emphasis on beat 2 continues with brass and timpani repeated notes.	
8:12	*Variation 26*	
	The staccato quarter notes of Var. 3 are smooth and rich here, in the French horns, then moving to the oboes.	
8:25	*Variation 27*	
	Sustained chords in the high winds, with smooth arpeggios rising and falling in the violas and cellos.	
8:40	*Variation 28*	
	Sustained melody in winds becomes more active; faster arpeggios rise to violins and violas.	

MusicNotes

8:53	*Variation 29*	Rising two-note figures in flutes, accompanied by syncopated string offbeats; ends with stepwise violin melody.
9:07	*Variation 30*	Suddenly f; accented quarter notes, with offbeats; slight slowing and ever wider leaps in the violins; four additional measures outside of the theme move us into the Coda.

CODA

20 (39)	**9:29**	Based on melodic outline of theme; increasing tempo; high violin line accompanied by driving arpeggios and tremolos; two-note exchanges between high and low.
	9:51	Trombones with two accented, compressed statements of the theme melody, punctuated by strings.
	9:59	Violins crescendo; winds play theme statements answered by orchestra; strings and winds in a syncopated statement of the theme; vigorous descending arpeggios weight the concluding chords.

MusicNotes

Giacomo Puccini (1858–1924)
Un bel dì (One Fine Day) **from**
Madama Butterfly

Date of composition: 1904
Duration: 4:32

Student CD Collection: 3, track 21
Complete CD Collection: 5, track 40

A SECTION				
21 (40)	0:00	*Un bel dì, vedremo levarsi un fil di fuomo sull' estremo confin del mare. E poi la nave appare. Poi la nave bianca entra nel porto,*	One fine day, we'll notice a thread of smoke rising on the horizon of the sea. And then the ship will appear. Then the white vessel will glide into the harbor,	
	0:50	*romba il suo saluto. Vedi? E venuto! Io non gli scendo incontro, Io no ...*	thundering forth her cannon. Do you see? He has come! I don't go to meet him, Not I ...	
B SECTION				
22 (41)	1:18	*Mi metto lá sul ciglio del colle, e aspetto, e aspetto gran tempo, e non mi pesa la lunga attesa.* [more movement]	I stay on the brow of the hill, and wait there, wait for a long time, but never weary of the long waiting.	
	1:44	*E ... uscito dalla folla cittadina un uomo, un picciol punto,* [slowing down]	From the crowded city comes a man, a little speck in the distance,	
	2:00	*s'avia per la collina.*	climbing the hill.	
	2:15	*Chi sarà? chi sarà? E come sara giunto, che dirà? che dirà?*	Who is it? Who is it? And when he's reached the summit, what will he say? What will he say?	
	2:24	[slower, with solo violin] *Chiamerà "Butterfly" dalla lontana. Io senza dar riposta me ne starò nascosta, un po' per celia, e un po' per non ...*	He will call "Butterfly" from a distance. And I, without answering, will keep myself quietly concealed, a bit to tease him, and a bit so as not to ...	

MUSIC NOTES

23 (42) **2:52**	*morire al primo incontro,* *ed egli alquanto in pena,* *chiamerà, chiamerà,* *"Piccina mogliettina* *olezzo di verbena!,"* *i nomi che mi dava* *al suo venire.*	die at our first meeting, and then, a little troubled, he will call, he will call, "Dearest, little wife of mine, dear little orange blossom!," the names he used to call when he first came here.
3:28	*Tutto questo avverrà* *te lo prometto.*	This will come to pass, I promise you.
3:34	*Tienti la tua paura,* *io con sicura fede l'aspetto.*	Banish your idle fears, I know for certain he will come.
3:48	[lush orchestral postlude]	
4:19	[final chords]	

MusicNotes

Gustav Mahler (1860–1911)
Fourth Movement, *Urlicht* (*Primeval Light*) from Symphony No. 2 in C minor (*Resurrection*)

Date of composition: 1888–94
Orchestration: Alto voice; 2 piccolos, 3 flutes, 2 oboes, English horn, 3 clarinets, 2 bassoons, contrabassoon, 4 horns, 3 trumpets, glockenspiel, 2 harps, and strings
Tempo: *Sehr feierlich, aber schlicht* ("Very ceremonial, but straightforward")
Meter: $\frac{4}{4}$
Key of movement: D♭ Major
Duration: 5:13

Student CD Collection: 3, track 24
Complete CD Collection: 6, track 1

SONG TEXT

O Röschen rot!	O red rose!
Der Mensch liegt in grösster Not!	Humanity lies in deepest need!
Der Mensch liegt in grösster Pein!	Humanity lies in greatest pain!
Je lieber möcht ich im Himmel sein!	I would rather be in Heaven!
Da kam ich auf einen breiten Weg;	Then I came upon a broad path;
Da kam ein Engelein und wollt mich abweisen.	Then came an angel, that tried to turn me away.
Ach nein! Ich liess mich nicht abweisen!	But no! I will not be turned away!
Ich bin von Gott und will wieder zu Gott!	I am made by God and will return to God!
Der liebe Gott wird mir ein Lichten geben,	Dear God will give me a light,
Wird leuchten mir bis in das ewig, selig Leben!	Will light my way to eternal, blessed life!

---

24 (1)	**0:00**	Begins with words of alto ("*O Röschen rot!* "), accompanied by low strings.
	0:22	Brass chorale: 3 trumpets, 4 horns, bassoons, contrabassoon.
	1:07	"*Der Mensch liegt in grösster Not!*" (strings).
25 (2)	**1:19**	Change of key. "*Der Mensch liegt in grösster Pein!*" (strings).
	1:32	Trumpets.
	1:37	"*Je lieber möcht ich im Himmel sein!*" Note upward swoop on "*Himmel*" ("Heaven").
	1:57	Repeat of previous line. Voice with oboe. Note curve of melodic line.

MusicNotes

	2:16	Oboe and strings.
	2:49	Tempo marked: "Somewhat faster." Clarinets, harp, and glockenspiel.
	2:55	*"Da kam ich auf einen breiten Weg;"*
26 (3)	**3:02**	Solo violin, representing the "ich" ("I") of the poet (probably Mahler himself).
	3:14	Miraculous key change, very quiet: *"Da kam ein Engelein und wollt mich abweisen."* Fuller orchestration: piccolos, harps, strings.
	3:32	Back to slow tempo: *"Ach nein! Ich liess mich nicht abweisen!"* (tremolo strings, oboes)
	3:43	Higher: Repeat of previous line.
	3:55	Back to D♭: strings, horns, harp. *"Ich bin von Gott und will wieder zu Gott!"*
	4:03	*"Der liebe Gott, der liebe Gott,"*
	4:10	Very slow: *"wird mir ein Lichten geben,"*
27 (4)	**4:21**	*"Wird leuchten mir bis in das ewig, selig Leben!"* Note wondrous curve of melodic line and the muted violins shimmering *above* the voice on *"Leben"* ("Life").
	4:50	Muted strings, harps; dying away.

MusicNotes

Igor Stravinsky (1882–1971)
First Movement from Concerto in E-flat
   (***Dumbarton Oaks***) **for Chamber**
   Orchestra

Date of composition: 1938
Orchestration: Flute, clarinet, bassoon,
   2 horns, 3 violins, 3 violas, 2 cellos,
   2 basses
Meter: $\frac{2}{4}$
Key: E♭
Tempo: *Tempo giusto*
Duration: 4:11

Student CD Collection: 3, track 28
Complete CD Collection: 6, track 15

---

28 (15)   **0:00** | Opening motive on strings and flute, with intriguing offbeats:

etc.

0:18 | Continuing on strings, with sustained dissonance on winds.

0:27 | Syncopated development of opening motive (see "Bach figure," Figure 1A), with "rocket" phrase on clarinet.

etc.

0:35 | Jazzy rhythms.

0:59 | Short clarinet solo.

1:04 | Fanfare: horns and bassoon.

1:21 | Clarinet again, followed by strings and bassoon.

1:38 | Crescendo: syncopated rhythmic figure in all parts except basses.

MusicNotes

1:52	Climax. Unison playing, winding down to:
29 (16) **2:02**	An extended fugue on strings alone; violas, followed by violins, basses, and cellos.
2:47	Louder, horns and strings, with fanfare.
3:05	New melody in horns, with busy, bubbling accompaniment on bassoon and clarinet.
3:26	Crescendo. Sixteenth-note figure in strings against cross-rhythms in winds. (See Figure 2B.)

3:55	Ritornello: slow chords.

etc.

4:11	Soft ending.

MusicNotes

Arnold Schoenberg (1874–1951)
Madonna from *Pierrot Lunaire*

Date of composition: 1912
Orchestration: Voice; flute, bass
    clarinet, viola, cello, piano
Duration: 1:47

Student CD Collection: 3, track 30
Complete CD Collection: 6, track 17

30 (17)	**0:00**	[Flute, clarinet, cello (1 measure)]	

STANZA 1

0:03	*Steig, o Mutter aller Schmerzen,* *Auf den Altar meiner Verse!*	Rise, O Mother of all Sorrows, on the altar of my verses!

0:18	*Blut aus deinen magern Bruesten* *Hat den Schwerten Wut vergossen.*	Blood pours forth from your withered bosom where the cruel sword has pierced it.

STANZA 2

0:32	*Deine ewig frischen Wunden* *Gleichen Augen, rot und offen.*	And your ever-bleeding wounds seem like eyes, red and open.

0:42	*Steig, o Mutter aller Schmerzen,* *Auf den Altar meiner Verse!*	Rise, O Mother of all Sorrows, on the altar of my verses!

0:57	[Instrumental interlude; change in instrumental figures]	

1:09	*In den abgezehrten Haenden* *Haelst du deines Sohnes Leiche,* *Ihn zu zeigen aller Menschheit—*	In your torn and wasted hands holding thy Son's holy body, you reveal Him to all mankind—

1:23	*Doch der Blick der Menschen meidet*	but the eyes of men are turned away,

1:28	*Dich, o Mutter aller Schmerzen!*	O Mother of all Sorrows!

[Piano enters, loud and abrupt with cello]

1:42	[Final chord, piano]	

MUSIC NOTES

Arnold Schoenberg (1874–1951)
Theme and Sixth Variation from
   Variations for Orchestra, **Op. 31**

Date of composition: 1928
Duration: 2:36

Student CD Collection: 3, track 31
Complete CD Collection: 6, track 18

(Read the Listening Guide first, and then while listening.)

THEME	

[Molto moderato ("Very moderate")]

31 (18)   **0:00**   The first appearance of the row (cello melody, first twelve notes) presents the row in its ORIGINAL sequence:

32 (19)   **0:12**   The continuation of the cello melody (next twelve notes) presents the row in RETROGRADE INVERSION (backwards and upside-down), beginning on the note G:

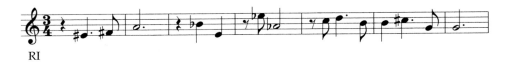

33 (20)   **0:30**   The middle section of the theme is played as RETROGRADE ORIGINAL (the row backwards):

           0:42   Gentle cadence.

34 (21)   **0:43**   The melody travels to the violins, which present the row in INVERSION (upside-down), beginning on high G:

           1:04   The movement ends very quietly. Conclusion.

MUSIC NOTES

[Andante ("Quite slow")]

(This variation features several instruments playing the main theme, against varying combinations of instruments playing melodic figures derived from the row.)

35 (22)	**0:00**	Main theme, clarinets, answered by English horn and flute.
	0:07	Continuation.
	0:18	Main theme inverted, played by solo viola, answered by flute and horn.
	0:26	Melodic fragments, all instruments.
	0:31	Flute, short chromatic figure, followed by solo viola playing descending line in longer notes.
	0:43	Main theme, clarinets.
	0:51	More rhythmic movement, entire orchestra.
	0:55	Muted trumpet chords.
	1:07	Main theme, violins.
	1:16	Faster motion.
	1:28	Motion stops, movement ends.

MUSIC NOTES

Anton Webern (1883–1945)
Third Movement from _Five Movements_
for String Quartet, Op. 5

Date of composition: 1909
Orchestration: 2 violins, viola, cello
Duration: 0:41

Student CD Collection: 3, track 36
Complete CD Collection: 6, track 30

36 (30) **0:00**		_staccato_, cello, short notes.
0:01		_am steg_, violins and viola.
0:03		_pizzicato_, violins and viola.
0:04		_arco_, violins and viola.
0:08		_arco staccato_, first violin and cello.
0:10		_col legno_, violins and viola.
0:16		_arco_, first violin; _pizzicato_, second violin, viola, cello.
0:26		_arco_, cello; _pizzicato_, first violin and viola.
0:30		_arco_, first violin; _arco staccato_, second violin, viola, cello.
0:35		Loud finish, all instruments _staccato_, with two final _pizzicato_ chords.

MUSICNOTES

Charles Ives (1874–1954)
Second Movement from *Three Places*
** *in New England* ("Putnam's Camp,**
** Redding, Conn.")**

Date of composition: 1903–11
Orchestration: Flute/piccolo,
   oboe/English horn, clarinet,
   bassoon, 2 or more horns, 2 or more
   trumpets, 2 trombones, tuba, piano;
   timpani; drums; cymbals; strings
Duration: 5:38

Student CD Collection: 3, track 37
Complete CD Collection: 6, track 41

37 (41)	**0:00**	*Introduction:* full orchestra with dissonant but rhythmically unified descending scales, leading to repeated notes; a vigorous marchlike pulse.
	0:10	*Allegro* ("quick-step time"): a bouncy, accessible melody accompanied by a regular thudding bass. The conventional harmonies contrast with the harsh introduction.
		Flutes and trumpets can be heard with competing melodies as Ives evokes the atmosphere of a chaotic festive event.
	0:47	After a fanfare by a single trumpet, the confused fervor of the different simultaneous events continues even more energetically, with strong melodies in trombones and trumpets, and heavy use of cymbals and snare drum.
38 (42)	**1:00**	Thinner texture and softer dynamics lead to parodied quotation of "Rally Round the Flag" and "Yankee Doodle," with:
	1:08	Disjunct melody in violins with conflicting piano and percussion, leading to:
	1:50	Softly throbbing cellos and basses, gradually slowing down, illustrating the child gradually falling asleep.
	1:55	Decrescendo, then quiet.
39 (43)	**2:06**	*Dream section:* Begins with an ethereal sustained high chord (the Goddess of Liberty), then continues with a legato but energetic melody (first flute, then oboe). But the regular pulse (percussion and piano) accompanying this melody accelerates and takes off on its own (the soldiers march off to pipe and drum). Different melodies in the violins, oboes, clarinets, and trumpets, in a number of different meters and keys, combine with a building tension. The conflicting pulse of the piano and snare drum against the slower pulse of the repetitive low strings can be clearly heard. This gradually dies down, and then:
40 (44)	**3:10**	A bold, new, brass melody emerges and leads to another section of conflicting melodies; simultaneously, "The British Grenadiers," a favorite revolutionary tune, is heard in the flutes.

MUSIC NOTES

3:36	A strongly accented and repetitive tune ascends in the brass and starts another dense passage.
3:57	*Awakening:* This comes to an abrupt halt (the boy suddenly awakes), and a lively tune is revealed in the violins (the boy hears children's songs in the background). This builds to another complex passage (different bands, songs, and games combine). Heavy, low rhythms and several meters combine. Fragments of lively string melody, "The British Grenadiers," and other tunes.
4:47	Repeated notes in trumpets and brass cut in suddenly.
4:54	Another swirl of melodies and rhythms, oscillating notes crescendo, frantic scales, as all the instruments push their dynamic limit, leading to the final jarring chord.

MusicNotes

Aaron Copland (1900–1990)
Fanfare for the Common Man

Date of composition: 1942

Orchestration: 3 trumpets, 4 horns, 3 trombones, tuba, timpani, bass drum, tam-tam

Duration: 3:36

Student CD Collection: 3, track 41

Complete CD Collection: 7, track 1

41 (1)	**0:00**	Somber strokes on the bass drum, timpani, and gong (tam-tam); gradual decrease in volume.
	0:25	Fanfare idea in a steady, deliberate tempo—ascending triad; then the fifth outlining that same triad leads to a high note and a slower, descending arpeggio. Stark, unison trumpets.
	0:54	Timpani and bass drum.
42 (2)	**0:59**	Fanfare idea, louder, now harmonized with one additional contrapuntal line in the French horns.
	1:39	Tam-tam, timpani, and bass drum.
43 (3)	**1:50**	Accented low brass take up the fanfare, imitated by timpani, then by trumpets and French horns. Harmony expands richly to three and more chord tones. Rising fifth and octave intervals in timpani.
44 (4)	**2:38**	Another series of statements of the fanfare motive begins. This moves to a series of stepwise descents from the highest pitch of the piece.
	3:04	A contrasting harmonic area is introduced, but with the same rising fifth–octave motive.
	3:27	The work ends with a bold crescendo but an unsettled harmonic feeling, evoking a restless spirit, the spirit of exploration.

MusicNotes

Pierre Boulez (b. 1925)
Structures I

Date of composition: 1952
Orchestration: 2 pianos
Duration: 3:26

Student CD Collection: 3, track 45
Complete CD Collection: 7, track 15

45 (15)	**0:00**	Sustained notes, use of extremes in range; although pitches overlap, few notes are struck simultaneously as chords.
	0:11	Pause, then quick articulations, some fast repeated notes.
	0:28	More held notes in low and middle range; a slight slowing.
	0:39	This section begins with a surprise—a chord—and has more use of simultaneously sounded pitches and thus a richer harmonic feel. The pulse moves forward and seems to gain momentum. Scattered notes leap about in the high and middle ranges.
	1:08	Low rumblings make a distinct line in that register.
	1:18	A series of stark, accented notes, moving deliberately in different registers; ends with staccato note.
46 (16)	**1:29**	Another held chord; return to a sustained texture, much slower and smoother, gentle and atmospheric.
	2:06	Sudden staccato chord moves into faster, more crisply articulated section.
	2:16	Another chord; others follow, repeated notes, playful quality.
	2:40	Pause; then held note in medium register leads to more sustained single notes; sustained notes contrast with staccato notes.
	3:08	Pause; then fast chords, gentle flourish of notes, fading away in a faint high range.

MusicNotes

Olly Wilson (b. 1937)
Sometimes

Date of composition: 1976
Orchestration: Tenor and taped
    electronic sounds
Duration: 6:02

Student CD Collection: 3, track 47
Complete CD Collection: 7, track 28

47 (28)	**0:00**	Tape noises.
	0:09	Taped whispering: "motherless child."
	0:35	More activity; manipulated taped voice and electronic sounds; echoes.
	1:00	Tape noises, both screeching and low.
	1:10	Sounds like those of a bass guitar.
	1:28	Loud bass. Pause.
	1:39	Whistle sounds, feedback, clonks, ringing sounds, chimes, blips, etc. Pause.
48 (29)	**2:30**	Voice and manipulated taped voice; noises. "Sometimes . . . "; crescendo.
	3:23	"I feel . . . " Tape noises; crescendo.
	3:43	"Sometimes . . . " Tape noises.
49 (30)	**4:08**	Very high singing, "Sometimes . . . "; much more activity, crescendo.
	4:33	Voice over bass tape noises.
	4:38	"I feel like a motherless child."
	4:56	"True believer . . . " Whistles, blips, feedback.
	5:17	Voice and distorted taped voice ("Sometimes I feel . . . ").
	5:44	Extremely high singing.
	5:58	Pause.

MUSICNOTES

Ellen Taaffe Zwilich (b. 1939)
Third Movement (*Rondo*) from
   Symphony No. 1

Date of composition: 1983
Orchestration: Piccolo, 2 flutes, oboe, English
   horn, clarinet, bass clarinet, bassoon,
   contrabassoon, 4 horns, 2 trumpets,
   2 trombones, tuba, piano, harp, strings, and
   percussion, including timpani, cymbals,
   tambourine, bass drum (small and large),
   orchestral bells, vibraphone, tubular bells,
   snare drum, and suspended cymbals
Duration: 4:01

Student CD Collection: 3, track 50
Complete CD Collection: 7, track 34

A		
50 (34)	**0:00**	Theme group A$_1$–A$_4$, featuring the strings and frequent punctuation by percussion.

B		
51 (35)	**1:07**	The chime strikes a sudden change. Sustained passage with high glassy harmonics in the violins.

A		
	1:32	Underlying timpani reintroduce the driving material.

B		
	1:47	The sustained idea returns, with chimes and an ascending violin line. This leads to:

C		
	2:16	A lyrical new melody in the oboe, with a soothing accompaniment including harp.

Oboe

MusicNotes

52 (36) **2:37** The restless, driving A material enters again, softly in the violins, and then building in dynamics and intensity. Brass and percussion add heavy accents.

A

3:26 The rising arpeggio idea (A$_2$) predominates, pushing the violins up to a high strained register.

B + A

53 (37) **3:37** Sustained idea, now dissonant and harsh rather than soothing, is interrupted by timpani (A$_1$), leading to the final, driving, accented chords.

MUSIC NOTES

Bessie Smith (1894–1937)
Florida-Bound Blues

Date of performance: 1925
Duration: 3:13

Student CD Collection: 3, track 54
Complete CD Collection: 7, track 42

54 (42)	**0:00**	Piano introduction	Piano immediately puts listener off balance before settling into a solid key and rhythm.
55 (43)	**0:11**	*Goodbye North, Hello South,* *Goodbye North, Hello South.* *It's so cold up here that the words freeze in your mouth.*	Strict rhythm in piano is offset by Bessie's extra beat in the first line. Vocal control: Listen to the change of volume on "North" and "South." Compare the heavily blued note on "words" to the centered pitch on "freeze."
56 (44)	**0:46**	*I'm goin' to Florida where I can have my fun,* *I'm goin' to Florida, where I can have my fun.* *Where I can lay out in the green grass and look up at the sun.*	Piano introduces a smooth, more melodic response to vocal. Listen for the added chromatic note on "fun." Note the piano "roll" filling in the space after "grass."
57 (45)	**1:22**	*Hey, hey redcap, help me with this load.* *Redcap porter, help me with this load (step aside).* *Oh, that steamboat, Mr. Captain, let me get on board.*	Listen for the deliberate variety and humor in these two lines. Each of the repeated notes is approached from below, creating a pulse in the line.
58 (46)	**1:58**	*I got a letter from my daddy, he bought me a sweet piece of land.* *I got a letter from my daddy, he bought me a small piece of ground.* *You can't blame me for leavin', Lord, I mean I'm Florida bound.*	Heavily blued notes on "from my daddy" ("daddy" means "lover"). Bessie varies this line by not taking a breath in the middle, making the ending breathless.
59 (47)	**2:35**	*My papa told me, my mama told me too.* *My papa told me, my mama told me too:* *Don't let them bell-bottom britches make a fool outa you.*	A new ending for the melody of the first two lines. Vocal line moves up on "fool," highlighting the punchline at the end.

MUSICNOTES

Duke Ellington (1899–1974)
It Don't Mean A Thing
   (If It Ain't Got That Swing)

Date of performance: 1932
Orchestration: Voice, 3 trumpets,
    2 trombones, 3 saxophones, piano,
    banjo, bass, drums
Duration: 3:09

Student CD Collection: 3, track 60
Complete CD Collection: 7, track 55

60 (55)	**0:00**		Introductory vamp between Ivie Anderson's scat improvisation and the driving bass and drum.
	0:11		Joe "Tricky Sam" Nanton plays a muted trombone solo atop a subdued chorus of saxophones and muted trumpets that blare out in brief response to each phrase of Nanton's solo. This solo elaborates on the entire tune *before* the band's initial statement.
61 (56)	**0:46**		Entry of the first chorus (see below). Blue note on "ain't." Note the call-and-response interplay between vocals and orchestra.
	0:54		Second chorus.
	1:03		Transitional section of contrasting character.
62 (57)	**1:13**		Restatement of first chorus.
63 (58)	**1:22**		Entry of Johnny Hodges's saxophone solo. Notice how Ellington's arrangement accelerates the shifts in the orchestral timbres behind Hodges. Ellington veers further and further away (in texture, harmony, and counterpoint) from the original statement of the vocal model in each variation. Notice also the prearranged backing and elaborate responses to the solo.
64 (59)	**2:43**		Scat improvisation by Anderson.
	2:52		Return to first chorus and fadeout by muted trumpets on the motive from their response.

MUSICNOTES

The Charlie Parker Quartet
Confirmation

Date of performance: July 30, 1953
Personnel: Charlie Parker, alto
  saxophone; Al Haig, piano; Percy
  Heath, bass; Max Roach, drums.
Duration: 2:58

Student CD Collection: 3, track 65
Complete CD Collection: 7, track 60

INTRODUCTION		
65 (60) **0:00**		There is a brief 4-measure introduction by the piano.
CHORUS 1		
66 (61) **0:05**		The tune is a typical bebop composition: angular, irregular, and offbeat. Yet Parker makes it sound melodic as well as deeply rhythmic. The rhythm section is rock-solid, though the drummer manages to be splashy and interesting at the same time. Although the chorus altogether contains three statements of the A section, Parker makes them sound different each time. The B section (0:25–0:34) is not as highly differentiated in this piece as it is in some bebop compositions, though its harmonies are different.
CHORUS 2		
67 (62) **0:44**		Parker really starts to fly on this chorus (hence his nickname, "Bird"). He also plays in the lower register of the saxophone to give variety to his solo.
CHORUS 3		
68 (63) **1:22**		The third chorus is unified by rapid, descending chromatic phrases, which in turn are balanced by arch-shaped arpeggios. A triplet turn is a common motive, and Parker plays right across the "seams" of the AABA form to make long, compelling musical statements of his own.
PIANO SOLO (AA)		
69 (64) **2:00**		Al Haig takes 16 measures for his improvisation, which is quite musical for a normal human being, but which sounds pretty flat after listening to Charlie Parker!
BASS SOLO (B)		
2:16		Percy Heath gets to play some different rhythms for 8 measures with hints of the tune.
DRUM SOLO (A)		
2:28		Amazingly, Max Roach manages to suggest the melody on his 8 measures. (Try humming it along with him.)
FINAL HALF-CHORUS (BA)		
70 (65) **2:35**		Parker repeats the B and A sections as a final half-chorus, playing with intensity but closer to the original melody. Percy Heath (who was said to be overwhelmed by Parker's playing on this recording date) gets in the last word!

MusicNotes